IN THE BELLY
OF HER GHOST

IN THE BELLY
OF HER GHOST

A Memoir

Colin Dayan

TRUE STORIES

This is a LARB True Stories publication
Published by The Los Angeles Review of Books
6671 Sunset Blvd., Suite 1521, Los Angeles, CA 90028
www.larbbooks.org

Designed by Tom Comitta

ISBN 978-1-940660-48-6

Library of Congress Control Number: 2018965696

CONTENTS

IN THE BELLY OF HER GHOST

How to Remember My Mother

I SAW SOMETHING on my left cheek. I thought it was a scab. I pulled it off. It was a tick. Less than a 10th of an inch and very light in color, it was a taupe little thing, not big and black like the tick I found on my back just a month ago. I was living in Nashville much the way my mother lived in Atlanta, but without her beauty or luxury.

As a child, I was in awe of the woman. She laughed at me, screamed at me. She shunned me, but now, dead, she stays close. Sometimes she comes down the wall like a spider.

For years I've been writing her story. Much of it remains incomplete, pages with titles like "The Lady with Camellias," "A Daughter's Lament," or "Blues in the Night." I tried in vain to forget her, but she has stayed around as close to me as my breath, hovering like dust hanging in the air.

After she died, boxes arrived from Atlanta. They filled the garage. I gave away her clothes, her furs, gowns, sequined sashes, golf shoes, and hats. But I kept my father's photos of her. There were thousands. One had been corroded by water. This photo of my mother just after her marriage shades from pale lilac to ochre to yellow to cobalt blue to gray, as if cinders were eating away at the remnants of color. Her lineaments curve gently in and out of the mold. What shows is one eye, an immaculately plucked brow, a bit of hair covered with something like a hat but more like a towel, pulled down with her hands caught mid-movement. The rest of the body is a blur of fabric dissolved into the waste of wet and dust.

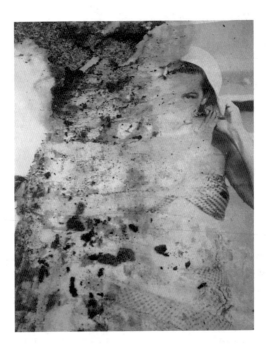

That eye — cinematic, hard as nails, her stare is astoundingly communicative yet closed off, as if letting us know: she knows what to make of us, and she knows we can't have a clue what to make of her.

Looking through other photos of my mother, she appears a stranger. I can't be sure who she was or where she came from. Everything seems make-believe. Anything is possible. She told me she was from Paris. Years later, in a taxi going to a restaurant in New York, she began speaking Creole to the driver. She smiled and told me she was Haitian. I'm trying to tell her story, as if it might account for my discomfiture in the world of humans. And yet as time eats away at the picture, I'm not sure it matters. She was a mimic. She was false. She may not be knowable. The story may be lost.

I always felt that I was not right in my skin. Everything, in my youth, had to do with race. What mattered most was the quality of hair, the color of skin. My hair was too frizzy and my lips too thick. She said I had murky skin and called me "Ubangi." Only years later did I take in all that the name implied: not simply a black, but rather one of those saucer-lipped women of the Congo or Chad, so distended around the mouth by a disk of clay that they looked freakish.

I did not look like her friends' daughters. She did not like me to touch her.

But who was she? As I write this, I remember how she hated to be referred to as "she" or "her." "I have a name," she would say. But even that was a changeable thing. Her real name was Sophie. She never uttered it, occasionally using "Sophia," but most often going by the name her friends gave her when she arrived in Atlanta, still speaking French. They called her "Frenchie." Like her appearance, her name was mutable, adapted to whatever role she wanted to play, no matter how fantastic. Appearance was everything. Sham was the core, the truth, and I tried in vain to tell the difference between fantasy and reality.

In 1936, the year my mother left Haiti, *Swing Time* with Ginger Rogers and Fred Astaire was released. It promised romance in the pain of the Depression: whiteness, a décor of stale purity, amidst snow and ivory staircases, ladies kicking up their legs and singing "Bojangles of Harlem." Fred Astaire in blackface imitates Bill "Bojangles" Robinson. Long and black, a pair of legs comes out of his crotch. Dancing ladies surround him. These legs spread out from him and over the stage, black and all-enveloping. Suddenly, women take hold of the black legs, pick them up and carry them away.

Then Astaire's white legs, his small and elegant real legs, begin to dance. No more Bojangles, no more black legs, no more mystery, and no more threat. Instead, Astaire became himself: the urbane man in love with the lovely lady in white.

After the dances for the vodou spirits, the *yanvalou* and *crabignan legba*, the drums in the hills around Port-au-Prince lulled my mother to sleep. And then a few years after digging in the Haitian dirt for lizards she called "zandolites," there she was, a teenager on Ocean Parkway in Brooklyn. She went to movies and watched the thin white dancer in blackface on a white marble linoleum floor.

My mother left Haiti two years after the American occupation ended, moving with her family to Brooklyn, where she met my father and soon married him. When the US marines finally departed in 1934, Haitians sang words in praise of President Sténio Vincent, words that my mother later sang to me — but only after my father died. "If there's anyone who loves the people, it's President Vincent," the song goes, and she sang it to me in Creole: *Papa Vincent, mesi. Si gen youn moun ki renmen pèp la, se*

President Vincent. In a deep and rapturous voice, she gave thanks for all he, "a mulatto," did for the blacks of Haiti, while ruthlessly punishing light-skinned elites. With this one song, she let me in on her secret: she harbored a confounding infidelity to her class and color.

Identifying with the black majority, this light-skinned woman, daughter of a Syrian merchant, used to belt out these couple of lines from "Papa Vincent, mesi," the popular merengue recorded by Alan Lomax after he heard it at the elite Club Toland in Port-au-Prince on Christmas Eve, 1936: "This is a guy who loves the people. This is the guy who gives us the right to sell in the streets. He gives us that because he kicked out the Syrians. So, we're crying out, thank you Papa Vincent." The self-proclaimed "Second Liberator" allowed the masses to sell goods wherever they could, and curbed the Syrian takeover of retail, shuttering their stores and driving them out.

Once in Brooklyn, my mother must have wondered about the sea, where it was hidden, and what to do when the snows came down. Nothing can have seemed right after she left Port-au-Prince, after the dirt, the drums in the night, and the mangoes she loved to eat right down to the pit, juice dripping over her hands. Things were so alive in Haiti, the stones that killed lizards, the fires that burned Jews in effigy, the gourds that held the gods. Then, three years after leaving, at just 17 years old, during her last year in high school, she was introduced to the most eligible man around. "On our first date I ran out of the car," she recalled. He was 20 years older. She did not love him, but she was the oldest of four daughters, her mother wanted to get her out of the house. My father took her to the circus. He tried to teach her to ride horses and eat mussels. I don't know what she thought about the circus, but she could not ride and, until her dying day, hated anything that looked slippery and lived in shells.

That same year, my mother traveled from Brooklyn to a honeymoon in Mexico. They traveled around for two years, then to Nashville and, finally, to Atlanta. The South must have seemed to her like a cross between Haiti and New York. "I would have been an actress," she told me. "Then I met your father." But she never stopped acting. She lived to be looked at.

After leaving Haiti at the age of 13, my mother never knew beauty or hope again. Everything that followed her departure and her marriage four years later to a 37-year-old husband seemed useless or dead. When she moved with my father to the Jim Crow South, she exchanged her complex racial origins for the empty costume of whitewashed glamour. I didn't realize until recently just how deluded she was about her real attachments, and just how casually — without really ever knowing the loss — she surrendered her origins to a mask of whiteness.

But in moments of privacy, when not seen by the eyes of others, she used to say things that sounded like incantations. "*Arab manje koulèv*," which in Creole means "Arabs eat snakes." I never knew what to make of this, but she was never clear about her family or her childhood, didn't know her own family history: her father never told her his origins, and told her not to worry. "It's no good to be too strange in a country you love," he sighed. She remembered feeling not "normal" in Haiti, that she did not look right to people shouting at her: "*gadé kochon pwal*," which she translated as "Look at her hairy pig legs." I heard her say this, but it didn't mean anything to me as a child — I made no sense of those words, either, in the dark of my bedroom.

Years later, I learned they were pieces of the life she had left behind, not just rapt conjuring. Besides "*Mesi, Papa Vincent*," she repeated, "*Desalin pas vle oue blanc*," which means "Dessalines doesn't like whites." Late at night when she came into my room, she returned to the pleasure of her life in Haiti. Her longing was consecrated most often in this homage to Jean-Jacques Dessalines, who proclaimed Haitian independence in 1804.

She praised only the fierce Dessalines — called "barbaric" by most historians — not the urbane Toussaint l'Ouverture, and not Henri Christophe. Turned into a god or spirit by the Haitian people, Dessalines is still invoked as a *lwa* in vodou ceremonies in the countryside. Rejecting things French and unconcerned about social graces, he fought to give land to ex-slaves, only recently considered property themselves; and when he drafted his constitution for the new republic in 1805, he took the most crucial racial configuration of Saint-Domingue and annihilated it. Instead of the three-part division of whites, people of color (or mixed-bloods), and blacks, he created one category for Haitian identity that absorbed all distinctions: Haitians, no matter their color, would henceforth be referred to "only by the generic word 'black.'"

In the South, my mother concealed her past. She remained estranged from the whites around her, even though she immediately recognized that she'd better become as white as possible. A gilded white lady of the South, that's what my father wanted. Confined by the role she assumed, she performed it, flawlessly. Hiding herself beneath a false smile and pale skin, she wrapped her discomfort and later her sorrow in silks and jewels. This denial of her history was not anything like a grab for white power and privilege, but rather a casual act performed in exchange for a lifestyle of luxury, which just happened to be white. This false if stylish veneer killed her spirit and destroyed any chance for happiness.

I can reckon with her life and mine only through how far I fell away from whiteness or how close I could come to black. "Who knows what evil lurks in the heart of men? The shadow knows." We lived, my mother and I, in a world that flickered back and forth between black and white, darkness and light. Nothing could be secure. She liked to imitate the shadow's voice. She must have heard those words — that voice, Orson Welles, on the radio in the late '30s. She would walk into my room and whisper, "*Heath*-cliff, *Heath*-cliff," imitating Merle Oberon's cry on the moors of Wuthering Heights. She became the Cathy who married the wrong man, died, and kept calling for her own true love. There were many women in our house, and all of them wanted something different. My mother became them all, only to realize that nothing remained alive inside her.

One day she pulled a magnolia off the tree in our front yard. She grabbed it in her hand like a castanet, shook it and pulled off the white leaves. "There," she sighed, "There — look — and see the red and the rot." I was astonished by the violence of that gesture and the softness of her voice. She was entranced by whatever had died and gone bad.

She knew that it had once lived in beauty.

A white spider too small for me to truly make out its legs came swinging down so lightly. It hovered over these pages about my mother, then two filaments came through the sunlight, now onto the desk, then around my cup of tea, then onto other pages, and now it comes toward me. Fragile and precarious, it hovers. I'm afraid to move: I feel that it has enveloped me in its threads. As if wrung out from the innards of her being, they loop me into her beaten promise.

My mother's past comes to me in flashes: fragments of Sinatra's voice, the sound of her laughter or the feel of her slap across my face. Now her photos, one by one, lead me like patches of light into a world that was but is no more. Not long after I brought them into the house, I smashed my nose against the jamb of a doorway, crushed my fingers in a broken garage door, and shattered my ribs in a fall down the stairs.

We found each other again when I least expected it; and in sight of her, with her breath on my neck, I know now that whatever mattered to me — the poems I cherished, the writers I taught, and the words I wrote — were inspired by her life and raised up again more fiercely after her death.

Haiti, Mexico, and Georgia. Bulls and skulls; drums and gods; recipes, jewels, and Scotch, these words shape and give flesh to her past.

Not long after awakening that first morning in Mexico City, she looked up at my father in what seems to be sheer wonderment. Or is it just languor in the soft light of a room sometime in midsummer at the beginning of their honeymoon. I had never seen any of these photos, all carefully numbered on their backs in pencil, and kept in two wooden boxes. Only now, with her death behind me, am I struck by expressions that I never saw in life, looks that astonish me in gentle repose.

Doom is never foretold. Not when you're young, just married to a man who adores you and takes you away to a place of sun, with dust, lizards everywhere in the cracks, birds wandering lost in streets that remind you of Port-au-Prince.

In Mexico, she heard the familiar sounds of suffering and holiness in the bodies of beggars and priests. But how bad could things be? A gold bracelet, given to her by a doting husband, encircled her wrist. She especially liked to see the statues of the Virgin that appeared miraculously on the steps of churches or on altars with candles, gold chalices, violets, and white carnations.

In 1939, right after their marriage, my parents arrived in Mexico. My father drove his Buick Special 8 convertible from Guadalajara to Cuernavaca, stopping in Mexico City, traveling along roads Graham Greene first captured that same year with his "whisky priest" in *Lawless Roads* and then a year later in *The Power and the Glory*, but I doubt they ever read him. My father didn't like Catholics. I do not know any details of their journey. No one ever told me stories. All that remains of the visit are photographs. They got there seven years after Hart Crane leapt off the *Orizaba* into the sea; just after Sergei Eisenstein began the film that would be cut and mangled in Hollywood; a year after Malcolm Lowry was deported, his life with the alluring Jan Gabrial a shambles.

My parents began their marriage when the New York World's Fair opened with the debut of nylon stockings, when Billie Holiday first sang and recorded "Strange Fruit," Judy Garland sang "Somewhere Over the Rainbow" in *The Wizard of Oz*, and *Gone With the Wind* premiered at Loew's Grand Theater in Atlanta. Franco had already conquered Madrid, ending the Spanish Civil War. They arrived in Mexico a year before Trotsky was axed to death there, at a time when over 1,000 American tourists a month visited Mexico, and artists too. But none of this, no history of persecution, no pleasures of culture high and low, no thought of politics can be gleaned from these photographs.

The suffering of bulls, yes, and the remarkable poses of my mother, but alongside a few scenes of peasants, cacti, churches, murals, or horses, there was only a young girl chosen by an older man, and continuously reinvented in split-second exposures, caught in hundreds of ways: lying down in a two-piece bathing suit on rocks, or sitting, long legs crossed doubly graceful in the rise of the stairs underneath her, or sometimes standing in sunlight, her head rocked to the side and eyes like tinder.

The bulls mattered, even if she didn't know it then. My father went to bullfights. During those afternoons, what did my mother do? As I remember her broken life, I can't stop thinking about the bulls, isolated from their kind, released into spectacle, performing their agony, the light in their eyes slowly turning into dark. The man rides the horse. He spears the bull and looks down at the stricken animal.

Three quarters of a century later, I look at the pictures. Out of boxes and other wooden and steel containers, and buried deep under other albums, these relics of a honeymoon emerge. They were not part of anything I knew, nor did they make up any kind of beauty my parents might retrieve from a past when they might have known love or passion.

I spent my life not knowing what it meant to love. There was no warmth in our house, no sign of a kiss, except once or twice when my father tried to peck at my mother's lips as if he was ashamed, a moment in time preserved for me now only in her grimace.

Lust I knew. The long afternoon phone calls when my mother rested on her bed behind a door that was not quite shut. Her legs I could not see. They were under the sheet. She laughed and sounded different than usual. Or was that love, as one hand moved up and down, and the other held the phone very close to the ear?

I wanted these photos to tell me something about their past, something that might otherwise be lost forever. My mother's face, caught in poses that were never off-guard or random, still does not speak to me. Sometimes she has that immaculate quality of being purified of anything living. When she looks out at my father, the hand drawn up on one side, sultry on the hip, I think of Rita Hayworth, her idol. The earliest films of this love goddess had been on my mother's mind long before she left for Mexico with my father.

Once there, my father said, the bellowing of bulls could be heard wherever you stood. The heat and the cruelty and the beauty and the grace were simply part of the landscape. The bullfight photos are large 8x10 prints. They touch my heart more strongly than I could have anticipated.

What more can be known about the honeymoon that left my mother cold, my father clueless? I am somehow sure that my mother never looked at any of these photos. She never had any interest in remembering the past. Her indifference to whatever she had felt then made her the woman that I grew up watching. I admired and feared her, but most of all I longed to be close to her, enveloped in the waves of her brown and heavy hair. Just a couple of years after marriage, the soft face of a woman beguiled became impenetrable in its exacting beauty. A veneer set in over her luscious skin. Hardness took over eyes that were once inviting, and her smile remained frozen for the camera.

That unyielding stiffness had not, though, yet set her face in stone. She was not afraid to be vulnerable, and her eyes still looked at what she thought she loved.

"Blood poured down the streets," my mother used to repeat after my father died. Cryptic, she never explained who or what she meant. Did she mean the blood of bulls or the blood of men?

She liked to hear church bells ringing. She prayed the words she learned as a child in Port-au-Prince, where the nuns at Sacré Coeur, her school in Turgeau, took away the girls' mirrors and then gazed secretly at themselves: "Je vous salue Marie, pleine de grâce, le seigneur est avec vous." Trying to tell me about her childhood in Port-au-Prince, never sure if she was French, Syrian, or Haitian, and light enough not to think of herself as black, she always returned to the nuns at Sacré Coeur. Her stories focused on transformation and shape-shifting identities: "They never told us about the slave trade. I never knew about that. In the beginning, the nuns told me, there were some little light pygmies that were here, and then they grew bigger and darker. I always wondered," she said, "how they got so black and so big so fast."

When she worshipped the Virgin late in life, she told me how God once loved a woman pure and without stain. Then she got confused, and remembered how hard it was to remain pure, especially when you hear stories about the *djablesse*, or "she-devil." One of the most feared ghosts in Haiti, the *djablesse* is condemned to walk the woods before entering heaven, as punishment "for the sin of having died a virgin." She laughed. "Think about all those nuns — taught they'd go to heaven, then they end up wandering around looking for what they never got or scaring the hell out of those who have it." With a throaty whisper, she used to say: "They get you coming and going."

In Mexico, her marriage began with prayers to the Virgin of Guadalupe, our lady of the hills and patroness of the Indians and the poor, so beautiful and dark, in a blue mantle, dotted with stars. It began, too, with the killing of priests, with the ice-axe murder of my father's hero Trotsky, and with a ride on a Ferris wheel that she never forgot. Each parent lost something that mattered that year in Mexico. My father, his revolution. My mother, her virginity.

Sixty years later, she recalled things I'd never heard her mention before. She kept repeating things. Round and round, always circling back to the gold coins she threw in fountains, the stones that hit dogs, or the sun that was always too hot. Less in sentences than in phrases, fragments, words thrown like skipping stones on water. "The sun burns." "The dust at my feet." "Two dogs bled." "Hit again with stones." "Gold coins, I have a bracelet of coins." Sun. Dust. Dogs. Coins. Because they never talked about their Mexico adventure, I had no idea what she meant when she called out these things at the end of her life. The photos before me bring it all back, her memories made into visible life.

"You remember how scared you got on our honeymoon," my father said to my mother one day when I was a child, "how you ran from the wheel, and it just kept turning, and you never stopped running." He said nothing more. Only now do I understand that he must have wanted his young bride to go for a ride with him on the wheel that spun in the sky. But he had no more luck with Ferris wheels than with the horses that so annoyed her. Only once did she listen to him. Up she went.

In Malcolm Lowry's *Under the Volcano*, set on the Day of the Dead in 1938, Consul Geoffrey Firmin rides with his beloved Yvonne on "the huge looping-the-loop machine" high on the hill in the tremendous heat "in the hub of which, like a great cold eye, burned Polaris, and round and round it here they went... they were in a dark wood." That feeling of entrapment in time that circled on itself, ominous in its repetition, the return of a past that will not quit, reminds me of my parents' lives. Perhaps their unhappiness was already fixed, in the image of a wheel turning, in actuality, and also, and around the same time, in Sergei Eisenstein's unfinished film *Qué Viva Mexico!*

All that remained of his visionary epic — mutilated in Hollywood — were three short features that pandered to commercial, and, some argued, fascist interests. Culled from over 200,000 feet of film rushes, *Thunder Over Mexico*, *Eisenstein in Mexico*, and *Death Day* were released between the autumn of 1933 and early 1934. The last, which Lowry must have seen, features the "Dance of the Heads." The Ferris wheel revolves dead center, while in the foreground are dancers, and three hovering death's heads, human skulls, whether real or masks it does not matter: not for this story of dashed hopes, where everything seemed purposely to turn life into death, but a death more vibrant than anything life offered, in a land where stone lured more than flesh.

The dead do not die, my mother knew. The earth was squirming with spirits, and at any moment she might be caught off guard. While she tangled with things too luscious to be put to rest, mostly the unseen, my father was busy using his photographic techniques to pin down patterns of light and dark, to capture brave matadors at the kill, people on the street, the *campesinos* in the countryside, women at market, but, most of all, his wife, transforming her into an artifact, as if her body had been raised up from rock and conceived anew in rolls of film.

In one photo he titled "Sun Worshipper," my mother stretches, head thrown back in abandon, hair a glossy smooth brown, one leg bent. Her body takes up most of the frame. With the mountains dwarfed behind her, she is so fluid that she seems to recline sitting up. Years later, it won an award at the High Museum in Atlanta. I remember my father's long nights down in the darkroom, after my mother had already turned her back on him.

Though my father never much liked to talk about their time in Mexico, he kept and treasured a heavy wool blanket with many-colored stripes, tightly woven, with the indigo blue, orange, and white lineaments of a face like an Aztec god. The other precious remnants of their time together were an elaborate silver water pitcher, sugar bowl, and creamer, and a large hand-hammered tray. As long as my parents lived, this baroque display remained in the dining room. It seemed to me heavy as lead.

In Haiti I was told that when you take someone's photo you steal their soul. Maybe that is what happened to my mother. Where was the injury? When did everything change? Hundreds, no, thousands of photos: my father overdid everything. How many times must a door be checked before you are sure that it is locked tight?

My mother was holed up in a series of rooms, first in Mexico City, and then in Atlanta, at the now-condemned Clermont Hotel on 789 Ponce de Leon Avenue. Built as apartments, by the time my parents lived there it had become a hotel, the kind of place that would have appealed to my father. An online site describes the hotel's wildly eclectic clientele: "For nearly nine decades, the Clermont Hotel has accommodated everyone from white-collar workers to prostitutes under a single roof." Increasingly decrepit and seedy with the years, it was shut down by health inspectors in 2009.

It slowly dawned on my mother that she had been given away to a man who had better things to do than be with her. But what could she do? Everyone thought of him as good Edmond, kind Edmond, and he proclaimed his love while he left her very much alone. What I thought was her wildness and icy contempt was nothing but revenge, one long steady erosion of feeling — or was it retaliation for what she believed he had done to her? I grew up blaming and hating her for behavior that became the only response she could find to what she could not control.

Though she could not put all this into words when she was young, she knew what had happened, felt it in her bones, and with every breath she took she sensed the creeping emptiness. He gave her jewels. She honked the horn of the car. He threw himself into his work. She went shopping. It was a standoff.

He kept her idle and adorned her so that she would be the most beautiful object in town. He prohibited her from working, when all she wanted was to try different things, anything to get her out of feeling that she was now more dead than alive. She found other kinds of freedom, or so she thought. By the time she reached Atlanta, she had confronted her own unreality. She was what others made of her. Everyone compared her to a movie star. A certain specimen of glamour, she was nothing more than a body that danced, her head topped with fruit-filled turbans, a Carmen Miranda or Lupe Vélez. Exotic, she appeared a lady of pleasure in the glitter and cigarette smoke of party nights, with men who leered and women who envied her beauty, even as they mocked her accent.

That's what I grew up watching, none of which she could tell me in words. Instead, I was punished, the offspring of a deadly marriage. She told me her pain by inflicting it.

You Go to My Head

AFTER I LEFT HOME for good, I would open a dresser drawer, and out would come the sound of my mother's laughter. Her laugh was not a giggle, but a snort and shriek. She laughed at Pépé le Moko, her poodle, when he humped the legs of visitors. I wish I had asked her why she called a randy, albino dog with squinting eyes and freckled pink skin by the name of Jean Gabin's impertinent and alluring gangster. She laughed at dirty jokes, or when she heard a ribald comedian like Belle Barth. In what my mother called "the back den," she played a motley set of records for her three closest friends — Zenobia, CG, and Molly: *If I Embarrass You, Tell Your Friends*, along with Nancy Wilson's *Yesterday's Love Songs, Today's Blues*, and Frank Sinatra's *Only the Lonely*. She loved his "Blues in the Night" with its warning: "My Mama done tol' me," and droned his lament for nature gone wrong: "The evening breeze will start the trees to cryin'/And the moon'll hide its light/When you get the blues in the night."

The ladies were gorgeous. Zenobia was tall with black hair piled high. Everyone talked about her drinking too much, but they said she was Indian and couldn't help it. She always stood apart from the crowd, though men circled around her. "Like moths to a flame," my mother said. CG was a regular item of gossip. Blonde and muscular, she taught me how not to be too feminine. She golfed as well as a man, and after the game, she always drank in the Oak Room, the one room at the Standard Town and Country Club that was off-limits to women. I remember she sat on men's laps, but I might just be imagining it. Her legs held a particular fascination for me. I have never forgotten the buoyancy of those blonde hairs.

My mother's closest friend, Molly, used to walk into the den, look at me, smile and say with her head tilted to one side, the voice gliding down like molasses, "Gone possum hunting." She was tall, too stout to be statuesque, and wore a lot of make-up. As a child I wondered why she looked at me the way she did and why she spent so much time saying "possum," which she drew out into a sound like "paws some," her mouth turned into a tight oval, pink and wet. "Gonna eat me some possum, ain't nothing so sweet," Molly crooned, adding in a lowdown voice, "They got pussy and the men are going after it." Men talking about a hunt, whether for possum or pussy, it didn't matter much. That's what she thought of their ways of loving you. Pussy and possum, that's about as close as I can get to my sense of the South: sticky, hot, and unusually cruel.

One night my father sat down by my bed and showed me a picture of lemmings. Thousands of these warm-bodied creatures were darting over cliffs and into the sea. He told me that they were lemmings, Norwegian, *lemmus lemmus*, who for reasons no one knew killed themselves by rushing away from their homes, running through the woods, and finally drowning themselves in the dark waters below. They appeared before me as if in a dream, a blur of fur and feet bounding down the mud bank and into the creek behind my house. I never forgot their headlong plunge into oblivion. It appears before me as something momentous and beguiling. My father always found ways to link what he reckoned as love and the death of animals.

Death hung around my house. No way around fate, that's what my mother told me. "Once something bad happens, it will happen again." My rabbits ate their babies. I buried my turtles alive, thinking they had died when they were just in hibernation. My mother's canary drowned in a glass of orange juice. My hamster got stuck and died behind the stove. A car ran Pépé down one afternoon when my mother left the door open. A neighbor's German Shepherd attacked Johnny the Pekingese — the dog we left outside — and bit his neck so hard that his eyes popped out. One eye was put back in. Everyone called him One-Eyed Johnny. A few years later Johnny was adopted by one of my mother's friends. She renamed him Precious, kept him in her bed with lace sheets, and told everyone he was her sacred lapdog from China.

Everything happened to the tune of Sinatra's singing, his chic and casual disregard: "Witchcraft," and "Those fingers in my hair." I took a deep breath. "That sly come-hither stare." Perhaps that was the problem. Even in a lament for a woman he loved now lost, there's a boozy kind of pleasure, a lingering sense of sex. I had a strange feeling in my stomach when I stood at the top of the stairs and saw my father in the basement taking what he called "dazzle photos" of my mother sitting spread-legged on a stool wearing a corset. She had ordered the corset and a push-up bra from Frederick's of Hollywood.

I began to repeat words prayed on the Day of Atonement to ward off evil and temptation. "But repentance, prayer, and righteousness shall avert the severe decree." I read Ezekiel and thought about dry bones. They could save me from the stench of flesh. One afternoon I walked into the den and saw my mother undressed again, this time right

down to her bra and panties, sitting on Bernard's lap, with a bottle of Chivas in her hand. Bernard was married to the woman who took on Johnny the Pekingese.

But there was another side to my mother, a woman who believed in undying love. "The Lady of Camellias." Not the woman who told me, "A rich man is just as easy to love as a poor man." Back I go into her voice, into the song she repeated again and again, only a few lines of it, when I least expected her to break into song.

> Our Love,
> I feel it everywhere.
> Through the nighttime
> It is a message of the breeze.
> I can hear it
> In every whisper of the trees.
> And so, you're always near to me
> Wherever you may be.
> I see
> Your face in the stars above.

In the sitting room of the Standard Town and Country Club, my father took a photo of her.

Set atop greensward with a challenging golf course, swimming pool, and tennis courts surrounded by woods, the Club was the Jewish answer to the exclusive Cherokee Town and Country Club and Piedmont Driving Club, which allowed only white Christians: blondes with long straight hair, the easy confidence of good breeding, a heritage of immaculate inclusion that was never at risk.

I never forgot the way my mother looked on Saturday night: diamonds, martini in hand, overly plucked eyebrows and tightly controlled hair. Not expectant or appreciative, but quite still in her elaborate, almost fleshless articulation of what should be ease but instead seems brittle, a woman hobbled by my father's devotion. Her face, though beautiful, seemed dead, as if the smile has been held too long.

The South was not kind to my mother. It lured her with what she could never be part of, a community of women that would always be closed. I look at the pale gossamer creatures with faces never threatened with sweat; and the lonelier I become the more I understand the texture of discrimination.

Sometime around 1963, I began to feel angry and mean. I was just 13 years old, but my mother's friends said I looked older. My wild, tangled hair and serious demeanor made me unpopular. Whether at home or in school, I never fit in. "You'll be left holding the bag." My mother looked at me with eyes dead as glass and warned: if I didn't want to "end up behind the eight-ball," which I always heard as "ape-ball," then "you better stop talking politics. Men don't like that. You look like a dried prune." I was alone except for an odd little boy who used to whisper: "I would like to know" — a long pause here — "if you would like to go" — another pause — "to the woods." To escape the lust of ladies and a little boy's lure, I spent my time memorizing songs from Broadway shows. Years have passed, but I still remember every song. When I think back to that time, I realize how much my life was shaped and determined by words like "I wonder what the king is doing tonight," "Let me entertain you, let me make you smile," "Just you wait, 'enry 'iggins, just you wait," "When you're a Jet, you're a Jet all the way, from your first cigarette, till your last dyin' day."

Now, sometimes driving in the heat of Nashville, I begin to sing and think how much my confusion about the difference between real life and fantasy began in those lonely afternoons in Atlanta.

Not just because of a fair lady, street gangs in New York, or a good-hearted stripper — though I liked to imitate Natalie Wood as "Gypsy Rose Lee," not quite taking off her clothes. Most of the time I pretended to be a dying swan like Margot Fonteyn, who soared with her pale, almost transparent arms rising high and coming down like wings in *Swan Lake*. Once in bed, late at night, I couldn't stop thinking about Christine Keeler and her pale long legs in the backseat of a limo. "Profumo," my mother whispered to her friend on the phone, as she reveled in the scandal that brought disgrace on Tory cabinet minister John Profumo. "He was nearly bald," she laughed, and "any man who looked like that got what he deserved." For the next few months, amid their drinks and laughter, I heard my mother and her friends talk about Keeler, as if she had once been their dear friend, a woman they admired for her naughtiness. They all agreed that she was too beautiful not to be destroyed by those who had wealth but no pity.

Maybe it was all just too much, the cottonmouth water-moccasins in the creek, the giant mosquitoes called "gabber-nipples" or "gallon-nippers" on the wall, the mother drunk on the sofa, the crickets rubbing their legs at dusk, the yellow and white honeysuckle I sucked dry. After tearing off the part that holds the petals together, I found the delicate string, pulled it out, and tasted the nectar like honey. "Kill the flower," a neighbor used to say, "and you'll taste something real sweet." He hunted possum, cut up snakes, and took the legs off daddy long leg spiders so I could watch the ball of a body bouncing on the dirt.

Here in Nashville, I remember what had seemed long faded away. It's enough like the Atlanta I knew as a child to make me feel cornered. Unease, a state of mind that is close to panic, overcomes me when I least expect it. Old rules of behavior beset me, even when walking down the street. "Step on a crack, break your mother's back." Whenever I see a twig, a piece of paper, anything at all on a crack, I stop and move it with my foot, as nonchalantly as I can. Seeing spiders that appear in all shapes and sizes, I know with absolute certainty that if I kill one, I'll be punished. "Don't you kill that spider if you want to live," Lucille said. Wedged in the corners of windows or dropping down before me, they hang in the air, whether dead or alive no matter. They're everywhere.

In the South, domesticity and chatter and ease are almost always accompanied by something gross. The sweetest memory depends on the shattered life of whatever is granted neither leisure nor mercy. In Atlanta, "the city too busy to hate," Lester Maddox took up the Confederate flag, iron skillets, and axe handles at his Pickrick Restaurant to block "colored folk" or those he called "heathen rascals" and "race mixers" from entry. During the first lunch counter sit-ins, my father's friend Charlie Lebedin dragged the Reverend Ashton Jones by his feet, across the floor and out the door of his Leb's restaurant at 66 Luckie Street, on the corner of Forsyth. He paid white crackers to kick and spit at black student protestors; then he turned off the lights and locked the demonstrators inside. My anger about this further divided me from my parents, who tried to ignore it all, and I watched their irritation with me turn to disdain. They didn't want me around.

I was 13 when Martin Luther King, Jr. wrote his letter from the Birmingham jail, and four girls died in the 16th Street Baptist Church bombing there, when John F. Kennedy was assassinated in Dallas and Ngo Dinh Diem in Saigon. Malcolm X suffered Elijah Muhammad's discipline of public silence after he described Kennedy's murder as a case of "the chickens coming home to roost." A week after his assassination, Liberace in satin and diamonds appeared with Cassius Clay on The Jack Paar Show. Clay had not yet become Mohammed Ali. But in 1964, after he punched out Sonny Liston in six rounds, I danced through the house, jumped up and down, shouting: "I am the greatest." "

Only two people mattered to me, and they are still on my mind: Thomas, the yardman who killed the chickens I had raised at my father's command, and Lucille, the woman who raised me, and, I almost wrote, "the love of my life." So, it's done. I've said it. She is close by even now. When she walked into our house in Atlanta for her interview, I was just a baby, and my mother used to tell me how I climbed up into her lap and clung to her like a "barnacle" that couldn't be "pried off." If it hadn't been for her, I would be dead. I'm sure of it.

I hear my mother ringing the bronze bell my father brought back from Czechoslovakia in 1946. In the morning when she awakened, she called for Lucille to bring her breakfast in bed. I still see the little peeing boy and hear the tinkling sound of the bell, a "bronze replica," my father said, "of the main fountain in the center of Prague."

Taking photos satisfied my father's sense of control, photos of the peeing boy and my smiling mother, of a beggar on the curb in the Bowery and women bending down as they scrubbed their clothes on the rocks in Mexico.

Lucille stood up to him. Lucille gave me joy. She walked around the house humming. Outside on a late spring afternoon, she spoke out loud the names of bushes, flowers, trees, and vines. We talked about lightning bugs, black widow spiders, daddy long legs, dried-out shells of June bugs left on trees, the difference between crickets and cicadas. She taught me the kind of dread that was also desire: the longing to go out of this world and know what can't be seen. She brought ghosts into my bedroom, the dead man in the closet, the white woman who appeared trying to get her hand through the screen of my window. When the trains passed, she told me to listen to them and behave, "'cause they were carrying the souls of orphans who cried out in the night."

Out back, Lucille conjured up love songs that only I could hear. When she wasn't crooning, she taught me how to recognize the ghosts that mattered most to her: little girls bit by spiders, husbands whose legs were torn off by scythes in the field or lost in the wheels of cotton mills, white women whom lust had worn down like the heels of her shoes.

One spring morning in 1960 Lucille heard about the students from Morehouse, Spelman, Morris Brown, and Clark colleges. They were still sitting in protest against segregation at 10 lunch counters and cafeterias throughout the city of Atlanta. My father came home, mad "as a two-legged bat," Lucille said, after he couldn't have lunch at Leb's Restaurant downtown because of the sit-ins. Lucille stayed in the kitchen and refused to speak to anyone for three hours. She cursed those "pig-eyed juveniles" making trouble. Thomas called her a "house slave, who'd die with nothing in her hands but her white lies." She took her lighter, flicked it on and chased him, flame glinting, out of the house and down Plymouth Road.

A few months later, I heard Lucille tell him: "I don't want you round here, go on and get your fool self to Birmingham," which for her meant dynamite, blood, and riots. But Thomas never kept quiet. "You can fall in a ditch and stay there till I go," he said. He wanted me to know about South Georgia, where he used to make 25 cents a day at a sawmill in 1939. Before that, he worked as a sharecropper, but said he had decided not long after he'd been whipped, "cut till the blood stopped dripping," that he'd never work on a farm again. "I wouldn't tell a mule good morning," he used to repeat. Years later, I understood that this was his response to the dubious gift to freed slaves of "40 acres and a mule." At 82, not long after Lucille had died, he remembered: "You couldn't tip your hat to a white woman. You'd get the chair. They'd break your neck. You wouldn't raise your head. Did, you wouldn't take it down."

Lucille

WHAT DO I REMEMBER of that thumping rhythm, the bulging eyes of the peg-legged man? A lonely Saturday afternoon in the kitchen with Lucille, breathing in her wet laughs as she flicked the TV dial. I must have been about eight years old. My choice was Popeye in his white navy uniform, but as usual she controlled the channels. *Quick Draw McGraw* and *The Mickey Mouse Club* lost out to *Maverick* and *Rawhide*. She dominated always. Humming, she adjusted things and the picture took shape.

Out onto the stage came a black man with one leg. One peg. It was "Peg Leg" Bates. Oh what, I wondered, happened to cause such a sight? As always, Lucille told me a story. Peg Leg, she said, "felt too deep, his heart was too good," but the devil had him in his hands and bore down on him in a car on the road to Florida. Dang fool, I didn't want to listen, but I did. I didn't want to hear any more, but Lucille never stopped, never did stop. After the crash, no one came for hours to get Bates out from under the car. That was the story that she told me.

Years later I found out what really happened. The lights went out while he was working in a cotton gin mill in South Carolina. His leg got caught and mangled in the conveyor belt. Since white hospitals were segregated and there were no black hospitals nearby, the doctor cut off the leg on a kitchen table. Down South, nobody thought enough of a black man to send him to a hospital.

"Learned" me the devil, Lucille did: the white fingers of some woman hanging like gauze on to her car door on the road to Florida, bodies split into two in cotton mills. "I want to dance on this peg, and I want to be good at it," the one-legged dancing man, filled with grace, was tough enough to say: "When I swing this peg around….You'll think that I'm Fred Astaire." No Bojangles shenanigans for Peg Leg Bates. Even if he had to wear black face to perform in a white theater on Broadway, he did what he had to do; and he did it well, tap-dancing with high-rising seriousness. The first black to appear on the Ed Sullivan Show in 1950, he appeared 21 times, more than any other tap dancer. When he made his final appearance in 1955 — he must have been around 60 — Lucille and I were together watching. That's how I remember him so well. He was another one of her heroes, and for a long time I could hear that tap-tap-tapping and remember him in his white suit with the white peg.

Lucille told me bedtime stories. My bedroom, with its twin beds and old mahogany dresser, painted an odd kind of ultramarine blue, with a cream-colored carpet, turned into my little cabinet of horrors. Lucille's stories were not fairy tales. They scared me out of my wits. She always saved her favorite one for last, repeated but sometimes with a slight change in her warning. "Stay on your back," she said, "or else that man in the closet will fall out straight down over you." I knew I had to be ready. Surprise could kill me. I would die of the shock, she said, "You'll wake up plumb dead, dead as a doornail. And don't you go screaming out for me.

Don't yell. He'll be flat over you before you can holler." Just like the spiders under the bed, the moon outside the window, and the hand through the screen, the man in the closet was waiting for me to turn the wrong way, look over the wrong shoulder, or say the wrong thing.

Everybody was always dying around Lucille. A black widow spider bit her niece, and she died a few days later. Her name was Helen. Lucille's first husband fell or was pushed off a truck and died. Another one was cutting Florida cane and the scythe slit his foot clean to the ankle. When she laughed and clapped her hands talking about the next husband, the only man she ever loved, I learned how terror could be jubilation. Like Peg Leg Bates, he got caught in a cotton mill, but he lost everything from the trunk on down. Cut just about clean in half. She was called in to identify him. There was nothing left but his chest and head.

Joe Moses was the last of Lucille's five husbands. I figured she must have loved him, since she changed her last name from Nero to Moses. She told me that she never "took on no man's name. Not until Joe." I only met him once, but like so much else in my past, I don't remember anything except what Lucille told me.

He drank too much, and Lucille finally decided that she would "fix" him once and for all. She was tired of the way he embarrassed her by yelling out the windows all hours of the night and bothering the neighbors. "Lord, I'm gone again," he would shout. When he wasn't hollering out the window, he used to jump up and down on the bed and hooted all the same. They had twin beds pushed together. So one night he jumped up, and she kicked his bed out from under him. "Lord, I done missed the bed that time," Lucille remembered him saying. She told the story with a wistful smile on her face. "He hurt his self, bad. Real bad. Went to the hospital and died a couple weeks later."

Sometimes when I walk down the hallway in my house, I catch myself moving like Lucille. Up and down I pump my shoulders. I hold my arms out, each hand clenched, dancing just the way she did out in the backyard, singing B.B. King's "Why I Sing the Blues." Lucille used to tell me that she was named after his guitar, though now I realize that couldn't be right, since she'd been around quite a few years before he named it.

During my third year in college, my father and mother wrote me that Lucille was old, so they "let her go." That's how they put it when they wrote me. She moved to her sister Nellie's house on Ponce de Leon Boulevard near Georgia Baptist Hospital, where I visited her my next time at home. Photos of me were on her night table and the living-room wall. She saw me looking at them, and said: "You're my baby, always was and always will be." We sat together for hours one afternoon in her room that smelled of soapsuds, honey, and the cod-liver oil that she swore by, taking it by the teaspoon whenever she felt her blood pressure rising. I thought then that I would remember everything about our talk. But memory fails me. All that remains is that smell and the feel of lanolin in her hair. Only in retrospect do I realize that I never asked her about her parents nor did I ever find out where she came from. No last words. Not a thing I can recall doing, ever, that might square with her love for me.

A few months later, I came home for her funeral. She had died of a heart attack, alone in the shower. Stubborn and tough as always, she didn't listen to Nellie's order that she shower or bathe only when someone else was in the house. Whoever embalmed her had the last say. That was a shame. Lucille never liked cosmetics and thought makeup was for "fool women." She didn't want anything unnatural touching her skin. But there she lay, in a suit, with a shiny black wig and her face caked with makeup. Even Thomas didn't think she looked good and warned me when I said

I wanted to see her: "You wouldn't want to see her in the fashion she'd come back in. In the clothes she was put away in." When the preacher asked for remembrances, I went up to the pulpit. I can't recall what I said.

"*Adonay shammah*." "The Lord is there." In his vision Ezekiel prophesies the future temple by remembering the first one, the House of God. When I think about the glory and gold of Solomon's temple, and its desecration, which my father mourned until his dying day, I remember what Lucille told me the year before she died. "You can find God in an outhouse hole."

I grieve for her soft, tenderly luscious voice.

Lucille died. My story begins. She was never gone, but stayed with me in the dirt or in the wind, surprising me just when I thought I had survived the night terrors. She appeared in all kinds of places, at the top of stairs, on a dark street, at a bus stop, down the hallway, in front of the bed where I had just been with the man I loved. She came before me just as she told me she would. "I'll return like you remember me. I got my flesh but it shines like the skin of a baby. I'll stand there in a suit much too large for me. Sniffing the air, I'll be real quiet and carry my night-time headscarf in my hand."

Lucille's ghosts uplifted me when things got tough. My parents disowned me, just as I turned 20, on the shore at Old Saybrook, for being a communist. When they sold my horse and gave away anything I had left in Atlanta, I gathered myself into the straight-up stance that I knew from Lucille, head high and sure-footed. I thought about the dead who did not die. What would it be like, I wondered, if the woman with the long white hand reached out to me from under the ground. The niece who died from the bite of the black widow spider in the attic kept me company, returning at night with her hand over her heart.

Lucille believed that the meanest ghost carried glory in its breath. She saved me from the Lord's fury, even though she scared the living daylights out of me. While my father warned me not to talk about the voice of God and his favorite prophet Ezekiel's chariot, which the prophet was not supposed to reveal — wheels within wheels, "the spirit of the living creatures was in the wheels" — Lucille brought mystery right down beside me. I could feel the fleshy wheels and smell the perfumed oil in between ruby stones. "What you gonna do when death comes creepin' in your room," she asked me one Saturday afternoon. I told her I would ask God to forgive me and bless His name. She said that I'd do better to say nothing and just get ready for the ride to the other side. "Dem bones, dem bones," she said. "Dem dry bones."

That day I heard for the first time "Swing Low Sweet Chariot." She sang it easy and slow.

"Swing Low Sweet Chariot, comin' for to carry me home."

The chariot didn't swing down from heaven. I never knew what direction it made for.

"Rockin' Lord, rockin' Lord."

Not up, not down. Instead the chariot moved back and forth, a rocky boat going across the waters to an eternal shore.

"If you get there before I do, comin' for to carry me home, tell all my friends I'll be comin' there too, comin' for to carry me home."

I knew that some people might get there before me, but once I got across the river, then I'd be blessed anyway, Lucille said. They'd all be waiting for me.

I knew Lucille was with me, when I turned color in Jamaica, proud when people called me "high brown" or "red" and committed acts of love in every conceivable way in New York. I returned to Atlanta, engaged to the man my roommate called the "hometown honey," got married in a big ceremony and passed out drunk at the reception in the lobby of the Standard Club. I heard Lucille's voice coming out of the walls. "My baby, my baby, what they done to my baby? They done killed my baby." She always warned me that marriage was like a "noose on your neck." The family doctor shouted: "There ain't nothing wrong with her, she's just drunk." My husband, who had been on his knees next to me throughout the commotion, later carried me up the stairs of our apartment in Ansley Park, just like Rhett Butler, I thought. Our honeymoon lasted a month, the marriage three or four. I can't remember.

A photo on the Yorkshire moors, early in the first month of my escape from Atlanta, shows me in thrall to the winds, though my husband took it to be passion. "To burn always with this hard gem-like flame" was still my mantra. If I couldn't take Walter Pater at his word and "maintain this ecstasy," then there would be no reason to stay married. So I left him. I ran to New York and returned to the love I had left behind, only to leave him too. I got ready for a rundown try for oblivion.

Make Me Immortal with a Kiss

WHO WAS THE SACRIFICE: my mother or me? Who was the scapegoat? I'm not thinking about the first goat that was sacrificed by the priest in Leviticus, but the one led out into the wilderness, far from the city. The scapegoat wandered alone with a rope around her neck, trying to find her way home. According to Rashi, the medieval rabbi and commentator, the goat, bearing the sins of the Israelites, perished, either falling off or thrown down a cliff. My father taught me the Jewish law.

I drew pictures of crosses on tombs and painted angels in a blue sky hovering over Christ crucified. What my father called fairy tales.

I wanted to be purified and gripped by whatever defied the ease of normalcy. I wanted whatever defied what my father valued most: happiness and security. He wanted me to go to Agnes Scott or Sweet Briar, where I would learn how to properly lift luggage onto a rack. Such a goal could be reached in no more than two years, he assured me. He nixed my plans to attend Sarah Lawrence or Swarthmore. Mt. Holyoke and Smith remained the only choices he would accept. I was lucky, since we visited Northampton on what was known as "Fathers' Weekend." Daughters and dads could spend two days together, eating, drinking, and dancing with no mothers around. That was enough for him. He chose Smith. Fathers' weekend didn't last long after I arrived. I heard stories about girls who tried to commit suicide after they saw their fathers dancing with their roommates.

What I used to consider my real life began there. Snow and Nietzsche; Yorkshire pudding and costly grace. Women talked about politics and not just men and marriage, though the President announced proudly to the freshman class: "98 percent of our faculty are men." In winter, when the air was pure and cold, I walked barefoot up the hill by Paradise Pond and memorized parts of *Thus Spake Zarathustra*. "There is more reason in your body than in your best wisdom." I discovered Kierkegaard and a new way to think about Abraham and the near sacrifice of Isaac, not as an example of God's authority and mortal submission, but instead as something glorious, an experience of "fear and trembling." I felt as if I was on the verge of a faith that turned obedience into bliss. Pleasure and prayer came together; and such intensity of feeling based not on certainty but on disequilibrium gave me a new experience of love. From then on I understood denial as the greatest affirmation, a surpassing of flesh that made passion palpable and a path to the life of the spirit.

Domesticity was to be avoided, and desire was to be stoked. I thought a lot about St. Teresa of Ávila. I wanted to become a nun and experience belief as if it were as real as a fist to the stomach. St. Paul knew that there is no renunciation of the body, and embodiment, whether clothed in blood and gore, or transfigured in glory, tormented me. I learned Latin so that I could read the Church Fathers, but most of all because I wanted to read St. Augustine on the Trinity. Anything that could be possessed was devalued. Only the unattainable counted. Fascinated by Solomon's Proverbs, I fashioned myself through a mind hell-bent on whatever was not of this earth. I surrendered myself to the otherworldly.

But that submission could only be experienced through the senses: a purely corporeal experience so extreme that it could become utterly mystical. Sophia Prunikos. Sophia the Whore, wandering in a darkness of her own making, suffering, and reveling in the paradoxical words of Hans Jonas, "laboring her passion into matter, her yearning into soul." In the fallen Sophia, the personification of wisdom worn out by passion, I found a way to join the intellectual life that my mother disdained and the heretical Christian mysticism my father abhorred.

I read to gather support for what I believed in, for the self-perfecting I was after. To love was to get as close to the ultimate as possible. Not just to burn with ecstasy, but also to experience love so absolutely that death was always near. Love-Death. I heard Wagner's *Tristan und Isolde*, and understood what he meant when he described the *Liebestod* as Isolde's "coming to clarity." Romance was nothing but a counterfeit if it did not end up devaluing the worthiness of earthly existence. Erotic rapture had to be so utterly beyond the bounds of the everyday that each time in bed with the beloved and every act performed seemed as if it were to be the last. "I could die now," I would say, "and not care at all."

I lived in a bundle of quotations. They were like amulets stored up against my mother's hatred and what I feared was a curse put on me. Some I made up and some were taken from writers who gave themselves up to "pure poetry," or as a professor of mine said, "chose text over sex." Now I can't remember which was what. Yet they all still beat in my mind: "bent on the bow of the Absolute"; "red like a burst pomegranate"; "the sterile woman of my cruel winter"; "I am beautiful, oh mortals, like a dream of stone"; "beauty is negative"; "dreams die once lived." "Love means ceasing to possess, but loss means possessing infinitely in the mind," Paul Valéry said, or so I remember. I made sure to lose again and again. I broke up with every man I had fought to have. I broke engagements. I contrived letters afterwards, vowing that I would never love again. Maybe I loved and lost so that I could understand first-hand the books and poems I so adored. But more than that, loving and losing became a way to prove that if love had to be excessive, its excess could only be proved exceptional if it was put in words. I was always crafting a story, and since any dream of love, once lived, turned into dust, I decided to treat each man as if he was some kind of muse who might offer me another chance to write about passion so luminous that it could not last — not in the way life wore everything down into compromise.

Before I met the German who took me to Brittany and got me pregnant, I wandered the streets of Paris. I thought a lot about doomed love, repeating to myself what I thought were Mayakovsky's words, his last words in a suicide letter to his love, Lili Brik: *le canot de l'amour s'est brisé sur la vie quotidienne.* A rugged sculptor named Gerard Voisin had whispered them, after he picked me up crossing the Boulevard St. Michel. I never slept with him, but I remember his beard. For 44 years I've kept the brochure of one of his shows at Galerie Rive Gauche on Rue de Fleurus. He wrote in large letters his translation of Mayakovsky's farewell, "The canoe of love is shattered by daily life," and scribbled here and there on its pages: "True freedom rubs shoulders with death"; "There is no creation without change"; and a poem that begins, "The poem is love realized in the desire to remain desire." Though the quotation from Mayakovsky was not completely right, it didn't matter, since the words reminded me that mere life threatened to bind and corrode the pleasures of the flesh.

It was as if everything I had read and longed for now appeared before me.

I shared an apartment with my college roommate on Rue Chanoinesse. We could see one of the gargoyles hanging off the side of Notre Dame outside one of the windows. I invited the sculptor over one afternoon, and she told me never to invite him again. He was an artist. She was a Republican. I left, moved to a little room in Hotel St. André des Arts on the street of that name, never saw the man again, but met the German. He was tall and blond, and he called me his "little ghost." I nearly died from our love when my pregnancy turned out to be ectopic. One of the fallopian tubes ruptured and had to be removed in emergency surgery. It's hard to give him complexity, or any character at all. Instead I see him always as he was years later, in one position. Serene and lanky, he sits in a chair, with sunlight coming through the casement windows of my apartment in Sheridan Square, unchanging, long legs crossed, cigarette casually held between slender fingers, a rueful smile on his lips. The words "lustig und langsam" — rollicking and slowly — come to mind.

The German asked me to marry him. He kept asking me to marry him, even traveling to Atlanta to ask my parents. Instead, I decided to go to graduate school, but first I returned to the South and got married to the man I no longer wanted so that I would no longer be tempted to defy my parents and marry the man I loved in New York. But none of these men matter, nor do the ones who came later. The performance of love turned out to have been one long and futile preparation for an escape from ordinariness.

It's not possible to return to this past without recognizing how ridiculous it sounds. But I was dead serious. Love unto death. I destroyed love so that I could destroy myself. During my first visit to a psychiatrist, I told him stories. There were many. I enjoyed recounting them. Once they wanted to marry me, the men were thrown over. The therapist asked: "Why do you hate yourself so much that you cannot love?" Then he expressed it in a way that was even more banal: "Whatever matters most to you, that is what you throw out." I answered with conviction: "No, not exactly. I'm elated by loss. I am obsessed by love, but nothing is worse than to watch that passion grind into habit."

Did I end these relationships so that I could be like my mother? She suffered with a man she did not love. "They clipped our wings," she used to say. I never knew who "they" were, but I knew what she meant. How could I betray her? "It's just jealousy," she warned me. "Always beware of women." No matter how much love I gave or got, I could not fathom where I was or who I was or why I should care. There was something blocked inside me. Was I accomplished? I looked at what I had done on paper and never felt that I knew that person. Happy? Not me, not the rotten little self who could never be comfortable at any social occasion. Not me, the person who could perform or teach or write, but who never sensed that any success was her own. The real me remained back in Atlanta, broken and fragile, listening to "the blues in the night" and "the man that got away," hiding under the sheets, and lying in the place of shadows where footsteps dragged across the floor. They dropped their chains, as they scraped their way to my bed.

That Old Feeling

FORTY-FIVE YEARS AFTER LEAVING Atlanta, I drove my car into a gully and herniated a few disks on a summer afternoon in Nashville. I tore a tendon in my shoulder. Then I got the flu, early, much too early, in late August. Recovering in bed late one afternoon, I saw a spider on the wall. I stared at it for a long while before falling asleep. When I awakened, I saw spider legs in the right corner of my right eye. Did it get into my eye, I wondered, hooking its legs deep inside as I slept? After a couple of hours, the legs crawled across my vision.

My mother has always known, still knows what she's doing. She wanted me to be glamorous, so I walk around thinking about her while channeling Dorothy Dandridge, the woman who most reminds me of my mother. Did I know or did I ever see Dandridge as a child growing up in Atlanta? If I did, I have no memory of it, no sense of her allure, no awareness of her talent or her tragedy. I knew the name but had no idea why. My mother, the woman of glamour who reserved a sneer only for me, adored Rita Hayworth and Ava Gardner, and later, when I was older,

Lena Horne and Nancy Wilson. I do not recall her ever mentioning or even listening to Dandridge.

Along with the appearance of the spider, Dandridge appears before me, as if in a dream, hovering in the early morning. My obsession with her marks how deeply my mother has taken me into her world, even now, twelve years after her death. The weekend after the spider made its home in my eye, I forgot about the Nashville heat and read *Everything and Nothing*, Dandridge's ghosted autobiography, and Donald Bogle's biography. This, then, I thought, as I looked at her on my laptop throughout the day, is what it means to love. Or to be possessed. Night after night, her voice wells up in me; and now there is nothing more bewildering than the feeling that I can sense nothing but her skin, skin that sensitizes me to everything I had lost hope of having in this life.

"That old feeling is still in my heart." Dorothy Dandridge remains with me when I walk down the street or stand in front of a class. If I put on lipstick, I think about her lips. When I run my fingers through my thick hair, I no longer want to make it straight; I am delighted by the wayward curls that never look sleek. How she entices. And for the first time, I know how awe becomes utterly down-to-earth, a feeling both extraordinary and commonplace. That transfiguration is the threat she works through and manipulates, a temptation that is also an affront, a come-on that is also a warning. She touches herself, runs her hands through her hair, and moves as if in complete abandon, while still, through it all, a sense of restraint.

Her ambivalence, the uncomfortable either/or, keeps luring me into the depths she courts. There is nowhere to sink into, no look or grasp, no embrace that might take me through to her and out of a world where people just want to have fun, escape into make-believe, or indulge in fantasies of hate. Dandridge performs as if giving her audience a peek into taboo made flesh and blood. Hating hypocrisy, she offered herself on the altar of blackness. She was more than whites bargained for, and they knew it.

She somehow helped me to return to my past, and if not to make sense of it at least to make me strong enough to face it. Too black to be white and too white for a black, neither black nor white, she fit nowhere. Knowing in her bones how race hatred, ever inventive, traveled from the South to Hollywood, disguised as entertainment — perhaps even more pernicious and long lasting because of that — she threatened. Her rendition of "You Do Something to Me" is a call to arms. In a game of submission, she blasts through her guise of demureness and hesitation, making a mockery of piety, with the dare in her eyes and the flare of her nostrils, with what she does with her hands. When she parts the frontal split in her long dress before striding forward among a phalanx of dark-skinned men, it's a severance as fierce as the parting of the Red Sea, and at the same time, somehow fantastically, it is also the consummate seduction. Even in her early three-minute "soundies" in the early '40s — "Cow Cow Boogie" or "Chattanooga Choo Choo" — she played her femininity to the hilt, even as she crushed it under foot.

Though Dandridge bears the trappings of femininity, she subverts the roles she affects. Whom was she fighting? What did she fight against? Blackface was still common, jungle movies scintillated, and a black woman could expect to play only maids or mammies, but she was the first African American to be nominated for an Academy Award for best actress, playing opposite Harry Belafonte in *Carmen Jones* in 1954 (the same year as *Brown vs. Board of Education*); the first to break the color barrier at the Empire Room of the Waldorf Astoria. She was the first black actress to appear on the cover of *Time* and *Life*. But even then, her appearance was a mixed blessing. The article in *Time* reduced her compelling talent and promise to the "wriggling" of a "caterpillar on a hot rock."

A skin of copper, bronze, honey, or amber, she carried with her something of a colonial curse — a heritage of mixed blood, an epidemic fatality that threatened easy distinctions between black and white. Imagine. Dandridge's beauty — her taut elegance and her louche sensuality — turned the idea of blackness into something so complex that it could not be laughed at or condescended to. How threatening that was to the quiet, quotidian white supremacy of the 1950s; its sure-fire malice came packaged as domestic cheer and wholesome fun. The stage was set for big black mamas or tap-dancing daredevils, and then she came into view.

Whenever I think of Dandridge, I become closer to my mother.

I knew Dandridge's world: the more you impressed, or surpassed the expectations of a white world, the less you were expected to do. Sammy Davis, Jr. could perform on the Las Vegas Strip, but couldn't stay there. At the height of Dandridge's fame and glory, she could not find a role in the US, though she persisted in breaking the color codes of the Flamingo in Las Vegas, making sure her band could enter the front doors as she had. In one haunting story, after she put her toe in the pool at another hotel there, it was promptly drained. In 1963, two years before she died, she introduced Martin Luther King at a protest rally in front of a crowd of 35,000 at Wrigley Field in Los Angeles.

Baubles, bangles, hear how they jing, jinga-linga. If only Dandridge's voice had reached me in the old house on Plymouth Road, then I might have understood my mother's fantasies of luxury, the excesses that turned our home into the stage for charades of love. Instead, I lived in the scent of perfume and sweat, an irresistible provocation that was always masculine. Frank Sinatra's Rat Pack, Dean Martin, Peter Lawford, Sammy Davis, Jr., and Joey Bishop, beckoned to me. Men got to be bad, as women waited, coiffed, and, it seemed to me, gasped for attention. When my mother screamed that I "should be like the other girls, like Molly's daughters," I realized how I wanted to become more like a man, standing straight and tall. I had only a vague idea of how marvelous such a transformation might be, but I can still sense inwardly the naughtiness. I was always left alone on the outside of what seemed to matter. But because of that breach, I saw and still see with a shudder the diamonds and painted nails, cleavage and crimson lips. I knew that I had to turn my back on such things.

Las Vegas. The Flamingo Hotel. The Sands. The Strip. Cigarettes. Booze. I could never square the joking lasciviousness or my mother's reckless allure with the torturous and trashy racism of whites. It's discomfiting, even painful now to watch Sinatra and Martin use Sammy Davis, Jr. as the butt of their jokes, calling him "Smokey" or "Blackie." No sooner did Davis finish his performance and time together with the guys, than he'd have to leave the hotel where he could not eat or stay and walk back to a rooming house in a black district on the rundown west side of Vegas.

But white customers enjoyed these quips — a ribald rite that was inseparable from hair-raising cruelties against blacks, whether by men in white hoods with burning crosses or through the harassing minutiae of daily life: the walk to the back of a bus, the drink from a dirtied, hardly running water fountain, the look that threatened, the walk on the other side of a street, a quick re-adjustment of direction, eyes averted, turned downward, the long walks to work where buses did not stop for you.

The hate, so dangerous and ever-present, has become ever clearer to me over the years. Maybe that's why I recoiled from flattery or any proffered romance, though I realize this is a sorry excuse for my discomfort with any kind of commitment. I wanted none of it. Always a dubious business, love for me stank of persecution. Rot kept showing through the dazzle. My mother knew it too. The rage, the despair of imagined betrayal. That's why she was always pleased every time I broke up with another man. "I'm here for you, darling," she used to say, cheerfully, adding, "You've got me. We have each other. I'm yours." When I visited her in Atlanta, in what she used to call "the ravishing dusk," she lay against her pillows with the phone on her lap, and I rested my head back deep into the other pillows where my father used to sleep, turned to her and took her hand in mine.

Remorse. Sorrow for all that I did to her, did by omission, the gravity of my sin: the grave error of the not done. Leaving her without glasses, once she could no longer see out of the ones she had. Ignoring her pleas that I visit more often or stay longer. I remember how she stood on her balcony adrift in Brooklyn with a caretaker who seemed to loathe her. As I climbed into the A-1 limo to head back to Philadelphia and my dogs, she used to repeat clichés that became her mantra — and after her death my haunt. I hear them still from beyond the grave, and my head becomes heavy: "Short and sweet." "Baby, it's cold outside." "I got that old feeling." Now when she comes to me, I hang my head low. I feel as if I'm a child, as if the horrors I did not experience but heard about or saw on the news cast a shadow over me, a shadow from which I cannot fully emerge even now on this hot Nashville day, with the glare of sun and the blue skies outside my window.

When I think about passion, I see her eyes. If I walk down the street, I hear her voice warning me: "If you don't stand up straight, someone will come and kidnap you." Getting dressed to go out to a party, I see her dressing for cocktails. Then she tells me, "Put on some eyeliner. It makes all the difference." My mother. When I say to friends or my husband, "She was so beautiful," I still wonder who I am. Lurking inside my words of praise is my own uneven life: the face that will not hold make-up, eyes that mangle the thin smooth eyeliner, mascara that smears. I've grown old and I'll die without ever being properly made up, and with every failed attempt to be more studied in my appearance — or should I say more put together? — I become more rough-hewn.

Everything my mother said, no matter how vulgar or superficial, has come to pass. Not exactly "left holding the bag," as she used to warn, for she meant left alone with nothing, out on the streets, as if a bag lady down on her luck. But I might as well be. My life, no matter how successful it might look to others, comes before me as a letdown; and even worse, I know it is a lie. In remembering my mother, I'm going to find the truth of where I came from and how I've failed. She was right. I know it now. But that's not the whole story. When she gave birth to me, my mother hired Lucille.

My mother won't leave me alone, leaving the tracks of her spirit all over the house, or appearing as a spider hovering on the ceiling and by the windows, with her words and taunts in my ears, but Lucille comes back to me gently or not at all. Sometimes I sense that her reticence and vanishing prove how much we loved each other. Her words still sound out in my head; and when they come, I cheer, I laugh. I am filled with her wisdom, always wry and moving me to know and feel more than I thought possible.

Maybe ghosts come around only when they want something. My mother returns to coerce, constrain, remind, but Lucille appears, and I remember a world without pretense or guile. As night falls, when the crickets start to sing and the raccoons or possums lurk out back, that's when I know she's with me. My mother leaves blood splattered on the ceiling of the kitchen — her blood, the drops that did not come through fully in her skin — while Lucille, who once told me she was, in her words, "your real black mama" — appears nowhere except in my heart and spirit.

How much of my past in the South can come through this remembrance I can't tell yet. But whatever happened to my mother, I know our lives take the pulse of the South, its cruelties and its grit.

I look out onto the neighbor's roof, covered by a gathering of robins. They start to chitter, and I feel again the onset of promise, the coming of warmth that I fear. Heat makes the birds crazy. They fly inside the screen porch and knock themselves out trying to find an escape. In the backyard, larvae appear on the bark of trees, and seem to feed on themselves, throbbing in a mass. Humped in the throes of growth, they gorge on their own flesh. Out of the cracks between the patio bricks come other worms. They leap or twirl out of the dirt and then dive back into the cracks. Some shed their skins. Others die shriveled in heaps.

Heat always comes with wet air. Folks call it humidity, but that doesn't convey the way the damp enters my pores and distends my skin. It bloats, makes it hard to hold on to any shape that might cohere as a person. I begin to feel as if I'm steeped in a brew made up of the chirping of robins, the sound of crickets, the swiveling of worms, the molt of larvae, all come to naught, all come to rot.

One afternoon, my mother appeared on the porch in Nashville. Her web was beautiful. She had turned black and much larger than the spectral spiders in my study. She always said that spiders brought good fortune. "Don't you ever kill a spider, because if you do, you'll see how fast everything goes bad, turns foul in your hands. *Souspiyant.*" I heard wonder and pleasure as she drawled out the "sou-spiyant," which she said was something like the stench of dirty water, or "something down underneath, *mango de dwèt*" — putrid or unclean mango. I remembered how she had told me about the nuns at Sacré Coeur in Port-au-Prince, and the pygmies who became slaves when they got too black and too big.

I kept checking on her and smiled to know that she had grown bigger and darker. But my cleaning woman cleaned the porch. The web is gone. My mother has not returned. If I came too close to the web, she would quickly move into a crack in the fretwork, then come out and spread her legs before me. Not this time. No more. I know that bad luck is coming. I am a sinner. Once buoyed up in the heft of that web, now down and down I go into the fire. Not because Jonathan Edwards's "angry god" dropped me there but because all kinds of gods had been waiting on the web's threads, hovering and caring for my mother and me before we were so casually torn asunder.

Little baby Jesus, Lucille used to say, "kept hid in those webs of glory," so that he could not be found and killed. Though she was probably mixing Moses hidden in the bulrushes with Jesus in the web, I always believed that these webs, wherever they were found, were signs of jubilation, never to be removed without bringing a curse upon the house.

Stéphane Mallarmé spent cruel winters with his "dear torture" and muse Hérodiade, "red like a burst pomegranate," but as sterile a woman as anyone ever imagined. Spiders quicken inspiration. To harm a "sacred spider" is the same as ruining a good line of poetry. In homage to the creature that spins threads of beauty out of its innards, he wrote a poem called "Une dentelle s'abolit." "A lace abolishes itself," it begins. Teetering on the brink of extinction, the spider weaves its net, as day becomes night and night day.

Somehow the air felt different.

I always fear the onset of spring in Nashville. Instead of brightness, blue crisp skies and rose buds, the skies grow murky. I call them "milk bone skies." Birds fly into hackberry trees. Native to Tennessee, the tree's bark is covered in bumps, or "warts." By the time summer hits, the leaves of the hackberry are covered with what some locals identify as "nipple galls." They appear like the cotton ends of Q-tips gone moldy and become home to lice that feed as more galls form on the bottom of leaves. Birds glut themselves on ripe berries, then digest them and drop what remains onto sidewalks and cars. Shit is the avatar of the new season.

My mother is not dead. She is here with me, laughing as she keeps repeating, "Colin, when are you coming home?" Last night when I came up the stairs, I heard her again: "We'll always have each other."

I knew she loved women, but always against a background of men. That's how it was in those days. She travelled with her best friends to Miami. They read Frank Harris's *My Life and Loves* and Henry Miller's *Sexus*. They stayed in the Fontainebleau Hotel, took photos of each other in bathing suits, reclining on chaises longues, their skin sleek with Nivea and Coppertone. Now I realize how everything luscious, exacting, and erotic happened when these women turned toward each other, whenever they looked away from fawning men and then into each other's eyes. Their smiles betray the secret. They felt pleasure in giving themselves over to an impossible perfection that could never be masculine.

Exorbitant pursuit of luxury and indulgence, exorbitant denial of what she most desired. Her unhappiness possibly owes more to what she wanted from women than what she lacked from my father. When I left Atlanta I swore I'd never go back except for brief visits, but she knew how to hold me, keep me locked into a life I could neither remember nor escape. She would drop an unexpected hint about her past, make herself into a mystery that pulled me closer, years after she abandoned me, paying attention only to criticize my bookish ways or complain about my frizzy hair.

Whenever I got engaged — and I managed to do it four times — she made sure to mock my fiancé. And after the visit to Atlanta, never able to feel the same about the man I loved, I'd break the engagement. I told my mother that the visit to Atlanta was always "the kiss of death" for my relationships. After the fourth failed attempt to tie the knot, she laughed and said, "the kiss of the spider woman." We were never closer.

I know myself best in the moments when I am most in her skin, unable to shake a familiar flick of the fingers, the way she held onto her wrist or said "hello." As I grew older, as we grew older, she clung to me, wanted me near and kissed me on the lips. I notice various cuts and burns on my hands and fingers. She always took things out of the oven too carelessly, ending up with trifling burns to her fingers or knuckles. Now I have them too. My handwriting looks like hers. I returned to the South and married the man who was just like my father. It was my sacrifice to her, the only thing I could give her that she would want.

"Get them out, get them all out," I can hear her saying, as she slams a door. I look toward the wall where a lizard had stopped.

She comes to me in dreams, lets me know that she's still here, in my blood. Brown pigeons still squat on the roof of my house. In the dream, I wake up and see my face in a mirror. Lucille sleeps on the couch, turned toward the wall to avoid the night terrors. I want to wake her and say something about my fear. An object lies on a bed in that room. A body covered by a sheet. It looks big. Suddenly a voice sharp but laughing comes from behind me. She cannot sleep because she is annoyed. "Why, mommy," I ask, "why are you so upset?" She talks about my father, something about his expression. Then I see her as she puts two fingers in her mouth to bite her nails, rubbing them hard together to show his nervousness. I'm embarrassed, but she leaves as quickly as she entered, a flurry of light and silken speed. In the bed a slow hesitant movement begins. The body turns to look at me: my father.

In another dream, I slaughter two people in a room, dark and stinking. I wonder how to dispose of the bodies. My mother is in the next room waiting to receive visitors. I tell her what I did. She remains calm. We talk about burning the bodies on a rubbish heap. Somebody's family wails in the distance. That bothers me, but somehow I lose sight of my mother. In the last dream I remember about her, I walk out into the bright sunshine after being locked away in some hospital or asylum. My father stands proudly beside me. I frown, afraid that I might see my mother — I worry because I feel bloated, and I know she's going to talk about my lopsided face. I fear hearing her. So I go to a cosmetician or room of mirrors to fix my face, to try and look like a person. I walk slowly by my father's side, the daughter of fears, into the room where my mother waits. She looks at me and starts to laugh.

The spider came back in my study. It was my mother. I knew it. All morning we'd been communing with each other, whether it crawled across the ceiling until it was right above my head or stayed by the window, moving its legs in a kind of jig. But no, it was hanging by one back foot with its front legs clasped together, and for a moment they pointed downward in my direction, so sensually and all a'shimmer that I couldn't take my eyes off them.

In my right eye the sprawl of legs remained. A strange darkening grew more intense by the hour. I went to the doctor. She couldn't say when it would begin to wane or whether it would fade away at all. I saw the retina specialist. There was no explanation for the spider, the web, or the legs that had taken over my vision. What I was writing seemed to have materialized in my body. The photos she took and the ultrasound show what was inside the eye. The blood vessels appear, and all looks normal. But I gasped, "that's what I see in the corner and across my eye every hour of the day: the spider web, the legs." What was normally inside, a part of my eye, had come outside, showing up literally as something external that covers whatever I see. It's as if seeing with the mind's eye — the philosopher's "eye of the mind" — had been made manifest in my body's eye, the actual organ of sight. The doctor agreed that writing the memoir might be a bad idea.

But perhaps it's a test of my spirit as I recall my mother, the woman who warned me about the evil eye, gave me an amulet that was a glass eyeball, and said whenever I did something she didn't like: "Remember. An eye for an eye, darling."

Once my mother came to Nashville, I heard her laughing on the phone when I walked through the house. Her low guttural laugh turned my gut inside out. It took an effort not to bend over in pain. When I heard her, I remembered ripping my dresses, tearing off the heads of my dolls, cutting their hair, and threatening to hang myself from the cord of the blinds in my bedroom. I also see myself in New York on a day when my friend had told me to stay in his big apartment on Central Park West. He was away so he gave me the keys and wished me luck writing one of my final papers for graduate school. My place on the second floor of 10 Sheridan Square was too small and noisy. It faced the Sloan's Supermarket and the little park on Christopher Street across from the Lion's Head. Alone in his living room, I poured myself vodka and grapefruit juice, drank glass after glass, stripped out of my clothes, threw myself on his bed, and took my pleasure to the sound of my mother's laughter. It came out of the closets, spilled out of the drawers of cabinets, and hovered near the frames of windows.

This memory remains sharper now than other experiences during that time. Perhaps it's because my mother always had a way of taking over my life. That possession of me is a refuge from whatever remains menacing. "Fever in the morning, baby, fever all through the night, you give me fever." I fell in love with Kathy. I met her in group therapy when I lived on East 96th Street between Madison and Fifth. Because of her I moved to the Village, in the days when Rudolf Nureyev used to hang out at the Ramrod, a popular leather bar, and we women used to go to the Duchess on Seventh Avenue South and Grove Street. Kathy received no letters from me though she was more real than all the men I idealized and abandoned. When my mother visited, I introduced Kathy as "my friend." Looking at me with a kind of grin, she said: "Sure she is." And added: "What are you doing?"

But she knew. We both knew. Unspoken, it became a bond between us. That pact demanded the disavowal of what mattered most.

They were either tragic or demonic, the women my mother and I so loved to watch whenever I visited Atlanta, years after I had moved away: Ann Baxter and *All About Eve*, Ingrid Bergman so ravishing in *Gaslight*, and Bette Davis as Jezebel or with the lift of her cigarette in *Now, Voyager*. Kathy was not beautiful, and yet I keep looking for her. She was the only lover I kept wanting to see as the years went by, but it was too late. I last saw her at the Algonquin Hotel in 1986. She was involved with another woman, she tried to help me choose between the job I had or another, whose only allure was that it was in New York; she advised that I stay in the place that I loved. I didn't listen. I was never happy again. Loss upon loss, and Kathy was tangled up in the bad choices. But in that tangle, too, we ran down Madison Avenue in the cold I so loved, walked on the old West Side Highway and down by the piers on Hudson Street, and lingered in bed, where we dispensed entirely with romance.

"Blood will run in the streets," Arkansas Governor Orval Faubus declared on the day the nine teenagers entered Central High in 1957. They were going to take their first class. It was their third attempt to enter the school. This time President Eisenhower sent the 101st Airborne to accompany them. White folks of all ages were protesting, along with the white students who leered, grinned, and held up an effigy of a lynched black child. I was scared. My mother told me, as always, not to look. But now, 60 years later, I'm looking. I see the photos of whites and I concentrate on the women. For the first time, I understand why my mother used to make faces at white women, the ones who worked at stores or took her ticket at the movies. These women were hard. Their eyes glared, and their lips were thin and taut. Mean, "like a rat in heat," Lucille used to say.

That look I used to see in my mother's eyes, the hate for me, it was nothing more than a version of what she saw in these hate-crazed whites. A domino effect, she passed on what most hurt or scared her, transferred it onto her daughter, a hatred she only knew because my father had married her and brought her South. The whole thing was cursed: the marriage, my birth, and everything that followed. Young and inexperienced, my mother had never seen cold and nasty looks like that before, so they cut her to the quick. She took them deep inside, practicing their hurt on me before she got older and gave them back what they had given her. In cursing and yelling at me, she passed on what she had once feared, and what should have been attachment turned to disgust.

The voices outside were pleasant and gentle enough. Just like real hate, I thought, the visceral kind that went so deep it could only sound like sweetness. That's how Lucille thought about those white voices, the "lying" kind: "Too sweet, just like honey, and that's what you have to know — women like that can't stand you. They'd just as soon spit in your face." I was 13 years old then, with buckteeth and frizzy, big hair, the hair that my mother hated. We were standing in the living room, looking outside. Try as I might, I can't remember what that room looked like. I see in my mind the old painting my father called the "Persian Sibyl," but can't recall the color or the shape of the sofa beneath it.

No room holds its shape or contains anything at all. Instead, I have the feel of a blur of things: a beige carpet, white walls, and a long oval mirror with a gilt frame. Wooden curlicues of burnished gold met up with a terrain of rose pink and fuchsia, though they didn't look like real wood but instead what I still think of as veneer, nothing more than a façade that covered over something cheap, and that's how I learned what it meant to dress up, to wear make-up. Where did I get my hatred of artifice? Maybe from Lucille, who wore nothing on her face and not, as she would have said, "one iota" — with the accent on the "I" — of jewelry. I can still sense the cotton of her clothes: a purity and warmth that seems to come from a place safe from anything fraudulent. How awful that I keep in my mind only her uniform, either gray or white, and nothing else can I summon to sight. But I can feel her presence, the touch of her skin, the sound of her voice, a voice that comes to me still, as a warning or goodnight so soft that I close my eyes, longing to go back into her arms. Nothing scared her, not a soul, not the hoot of an owl, the hiss of a snake, the glare of a white lady. I never forgot her favorite saying: "Don't pay it no mind." "Never pay her any mind." While my mother cared about what others thought, my appearance or style, Lucille wasn't "studying any of it." None of it mattered. Not when we had the dark woods and the storm-filled air when creeks filled with the sounds of frogs.

A dynamite bomb exploded in 16th Street Baptist Church in Birmingham in 1963. Four young girls died in the explosion. Addie Mae Collins, Carole Robertson, Cynthia Wesley, and Denise McNair. Resigned to the acquittal of the killers, Lucille looked at me and said, almost in a whisper: "Well, now what did you expect? Ain't no white man gonna suffer for murdering little black children." A year later, in summer, the KKK killed three civil rights activists in Mississippi. Lucille would hear nothing about the mocking, burning, torture, killing, of blacks and those whites who traveled to the South to fight alongside them. "You shut your mouth, girl," she told me. And she wasn't kidding. Lucille never cottoned to "mean ole whites" or even to the other whites she called "moaning so-and-sos," who whined and spent their time helping blacks. In her mind, it was all about sex anyway, and she knew the rock-bottom truth: "No hate like white hate," she warned. "Them whites just can't get enough of black bodies. One way or the other, they'll get you, pull you down, lift you up, till the sun is going down, and you still be working your life away."

She must have known my mother was not really white, but it didn't matter anyway, and she called me her baby. It was all confused. When Lucille and I were together, whether walking down the streets, sitting on the stoop, watching TV, or talking about dogs or men or trains, everything was all right. Nothing could hurt me. She spat at fear. "Don't want no cry-babies round here." She talked straight to me about men and how they wasted your time. She set an example, one that could make me proud even as I watched my mother and her friends. They were all so languid, as they listened with drinks in their hands to love songs by that man named Sinatra, who was what they called a "cocksman," ready to flatter and seduce. Lucille shook her head and laughed, yes, a laugh fine and deep that came up from down in her belly, not like my mother's loud chortles. They always seemed to reverberate somewhere between her throat and palate, hovering, hot, guttural, held tight by the gums, and clattering on her front teeth.

If We Win this War

"LOOK AWAY, LOOK AWAY, look away, Dixie Land… Away, away, away down South in Dixie." We sang loudly as we stood in Mrs. Guptill's fifth grade class. I was nine years old, and even now, as soon as I hear the first chords of this anthem, I remember how my heart swelled and tears filled my eyes. My father didn't give a hoot about the Confederacy and I don't recall my mother saying much at all about the Old South of loss and suffering. She had no truck with Southern belles, or anything to do with live oaks and gray moss, the red clay and June bugs of Georgia. But Lucille cared. It mattered to her, the beauty and the song. Everything was scary and magical. With her, I lived in a place that had a past like no other. That Atlanta soil, its creeks and every last tree, had a story to tell, and she told me those stories. "There is blood in the dirt," she said. "That's what makes it so rich." I learned about glory and surrender. Lucille taught me "Dixie."

> There's buckwheat cakes and Injin batter,
> Makes you fat or a little fatter!

Look away! Look away! Look away, Dixie's Land!
Then hoe it down and scratch your gravel,
To Dixie's Land I'm bound to travel!
Look away! Look away! Look away, Dixie's Land!

Who knows where she first heard this song. I never asked her. Instead, I listened hard and sang along with her. Anything sung by Lucille absorbed me and taught me what mattered in life, what was to be longed for and what ignored or hated. But most of all her singing taught me about sustenance from the gauze-like air in the summer morning, as well as faith in the dark at the edges of woods. She didn't sing "Dixie" because she hankered after a past of corsets and lace, but as an ode to the landscape she loved, the only soil fit for ghosts, "the only ground that hums along with the dead," as she put it. She used to say that if I listened hard enough, putting my ear hard against the dirt, then I could hear their groans. She might have despised romance, but she loved the South. *Gone With the Wind* fascinated her. She'd read all about it, adored Hattie McDaniel as well as Vivien Leigh, hated Sherman and "what he did to Atlanta" as much as any unreconstructed Southern white.

So if there's any reason why I get chills or my heart beats faster when I hear "Dixie" or spit at the memory of Sherman, it's because of Lucille. She gave me passion for the "Cause," lost as it was. I hate my own nostalgia, it goes against the grain of everything I believe in, though it was Lucille's nostalgia, too. Was that acquiescence, resignation, or just plain stubbornness? Did she feel attached to whatever devoured itself in too much passion? Or was it just her own soil, trodden and worked up by her ancestors? For her, the South was not its preening white people.

"I'm not studying them," she said. "I learned long ago not to see them, but this land is mine, and I'll be walking it till I die."

I wished I could follow her example. She just didn't give a damn about whites, not even enough to bristle if she thought about signs that said "colored" on water fountains or separate bathrooms or gas stations without bathrooms at all for blacks. What she did recall and talk about were attack dogs, chain gangs, white women, and the war that brought the South to its knees. She knew every battle: Chickamauga, Kennesaw Mountain, Pickett's Charge, especially the Battle of Atlanta. "That fight in Atlanta, it wasn't no battle. That devil just burned everything in his path." She then reminded me that when we went downtown we were actually standing on streets that were built way up high above the real Atlanta, all in ruins now, because of William Tecumseh Sherman, the man Lucille called "that Yankee cur."

When the shopping district known as "Underground Atlanta" opened in 1969, I learned that some of the buildings, now stores for tourists, including Lester Maddox's souvenir shop, were built during Reconstruction. Lucille wouldn't go there if her life depended on it, explaining, "There ain't nothing down there but Yankee thieves, and don't you go telling me nothing else." She even put my father in his place one morning when he confided to us that he wanted to open a store down there: "You stay right where you are. You got no business with them carpetbag men." Lucille was the only woman he listened to. His fragile authoritarianism gave way before her steady strength. No store was built.

I still can't quite fathom Lucille's strange way of idealizing the Old South. There was no war but the one the Confederates lost, and to this day I remember her hankering for a battle to keep the South just as it was, slaves and all. What did it mean to her, this place where her people were enslaved and brutalized? Somehow she separated out the slaver from the farmer, master from sharecropper. Anyone who lived close to the land, and felt its dirt in every pore of skin, got her respect. She ignored everything else about them. Though she called them "no-good crackers," she admired their devotion to the soil, even if it was nothing more than muck or mud. "That's something," she used to whisper. "It's what joins us together, even if they be hard and cruel. And Lord knows, they got that rope at the ready."

A gorgeous gala of cruelty, that's how I think of it now, the celebration for the opening of *Gone With the Wind* in 1939. No Hattie McDaniel or Butterfly McQueen in sight. They couldn't even be seen on the street walking into the premiere. Black audiences had to wait for months until they could see the movie in a colored theater. Lucille told me one afternoon about how McDaniel wasn't allowed even to be present as part of the cast when the film opened, when a crowd of 300,000 Southerners greeted the arrival of Vivien Leigh, Clark Gable, and Olivia de Havilland. "No negra woman could join no big party with whites," she explained. "The hate was that strong." Fame did not help in a place like Atlanta; if anything, it made McDaniel even more of a threat. All eyes were on Leigh, anyway, the deeply alluring woman with skin as white as alabaster and a waist so thin that "you could wear your bracelet on her waist," as Lucille enjoyed saying.

The movie was nominated for a record-setting 13 Academy Awards. It won eight. McDaniel, its black "mammy," was the first African American to win an Oscar as "best supporting actress." She was not allowed to sit with everyone else at the Coconut Grove nightclub in the Ambassador Hotel in Los Angeles. She sat, white gardenias in her hair, at a back table against the far wall. Ten years later, a speeding car hit and killed Margaret Mitchell as she crossed Peachtree Street. When I heard the story, and I heard it often, I thought it was God's punishment for writing a book that talked about "niggers" and glorified the KKK. Though Selznick soft-pedaled the terrors of the Klan in his film, we all knew the book. Our elementary school teachers had intoned the racist sections of the book to us for years. I can still see the embittered and fierce Mrs. Guptill turn nostalgically toward the Confederate flag hanging next to the blackboard and say softly, "We *will* rise again."

When I got home and told Lucille what Mrs. Guptill said, she stood on the top of the porch stairs and stared straight ahead as if she was looking into distant fields. I could not make out her expression, but inhaled the aroma of her skin. After a few moments, she walked down onto the patio and sang another of her favorite songs by Fats Domino — not the whole song but just these lines:

> I'm walkin', yes indeed and I'm talkin'
> About you and me, I'm hopin'
> That you'll come back to me, yeah, yeah
> I'm walkin', yes I am and I'm talkin'

Then she stopped, holding up her hand to shield her eyes from the sun and said: "And that's what you gonna' do. Hold up your head and walk. Walk like your life gonna depend on it." It was both dreadful and confusing that Lucille could be intoxicated by the strains of "Dixie" and at the same time teach me to stand up and fight back — "walk tall and talk back," she used to say, even though she knew that even to look into a white man's eye could mean a world of sorrow. It is difficult to explain the kind of distortion that such incongruous mixing ushered into my life. I found myself a willing prey to such inconsistency, torn between a singular, sad fantasy of the South and the need to keep on walking on the wrong side of white devils. Either way, I remained haunted by the chimaera of whiteness.

Just two years after Mrs. Guptill's class, *Gone With the Wind* opened again at the Loew's Grand Theatre on Peachtree Street in Atlanta, commemorating the centennial anniversary of the start of the Civil War, or as we knew it, "The War of Northern Aggression." I don't remember much about this other gala "premiere" in 1961, but I will never forget how eager I felt when, a few days later, Lucille dropped my friend Peggy and me off to see it one Saturday afternoon. We tried to peek into the Zebra Lounge next door, tempted by the giant marquee: "Beautiful Go-Go Girls." As I left her car, Lucille told me to watch closely and "don't forget a thing, 'cause you got to tell me all about it when you get home." Then I heard her mutter under her breath: "Lies and lace, lies and lace."

I watched the movie grimly, since I knew that Lucille wouldn't see it no matter how much she wanted. The Loew's Grand had no special section for blacks, so that meant no black could ever see a movie there. Only the Fox allowed blacks and whites. I still see or imagine I see the signs: "Coloured Must Sit in the Balcony" and "Coloured Parking." Blacks had to go to a separate "colored" box office window at the back and sit behind a segregation wall in the middle of the second floor dress circle. I'm certain that Lucille never gave such an opportunity a second thought. I suppose it smacked of what she called "shit covered in sugar."

Six years later the movie opened yet again, this time with lots of advertising and a poster featuring Clark Gable with his shirt ripped open as he held Vivien Leigh against a background of flames. That was the burning of Atlanta, and Lucille knew it. She'd seen photos in *Life* magazine way back when the film first opened on December 15, 1939, 10 years to the day before my birth, as she liked to remind me: "That sure says something. You was born the very day that *Gone With the Wind* first appeared"; and she'd usually add, "But you sure ain't no Scarlett." I never knew for sure if that was something to be proud of, but I figured it wasn't.

My strong sense of Southern femininity in the person of Vivien Leigh was banished by the unique excitement of amorous women such as Ava Gardner and Elizabeth Taylor. Both remain for me indelibly tied to the heat and raging landscape of Mexico — and to the men they left behind but always loved. But whether in Mexico or California, they carried with them always a rush of scandal and the fragrance of sex. Frank Sinatra left his wife for Ava. Richard Burton left his wife for Liz. Burton had been one of the greatest Shakespearean actors, and then he met Liz and "threw it all away," as my mother said: "threw it all away and made bad movies so that he could make money and buy her that Krupp diamond." The juicy headlines about Frank and Ava, Dick and Liz that I read in magazines and newspapers like *The National Enquirer*, even *Time* and *Life*, piled high on my mother's night table, took my mind off the killing Klan and my fear of their rallies and cross burnings, their warlike threats and rabble-rousing. But not for long, since Lucille made sure that I never forgot how, with every wanton toast of these star-crossed white lovers, came the real story, the one that mattered.

Clinking glasses of Scotch on the rocks and erotic misrule were nothing more than a dull accompaniment to crimes and nightmares. Lucille stood in my bedroom and listened to Bob Dylan sing, "A bullet from the back of a bush took Medgar Evers's blood./A finger fired the trigger to his name." Shaking her head, she told me to stop listening to such downhearted music. She preferred the likes of Wilson Pickett, "the Wicked Pickett," and she'd belt out: "I'm gonna wait till the midnight hour/That's when my love comes tumbling down. I'm gonna wait till the stars come out/And see that twinkle in your eyes/I'm gonna wait till the midnight hour/That's when my love begins to shine."

"What they done to us don't need no rehearsin'," Lucille flatly informed me. No one had to tell her about the nighttime knock on the door, about whites rejoicing as life lapsed out of black bodies hanging on trees, about the poverty, shacks, and bullets that Dylan lamented. Against such a charged backdrop, Pickett's soul music captured the sass and strength she loved, and all in the face of Jim Crow. Pickett knew what it meant to travel into the South, to be stopped on the highway by state troopers, to get out of the car, stand in the glare of a flashlight and be made to prove that you are what you say — and not just a "boy" — by singing for them.

A few days before my "sweet 16" party, Lucille and my mother had their first real fight. They had disagreements before, but nothing like this bout of screaming in the late afternoon. She'd been so busy with her friends, her shopping, her flirtations and travel that Lucille and I were always together, doing exactly what we wanted. My mother wanted me to be miserable no matter what, so she saw to it that anything that made me happy was stopped. She decided that she wanted this birthday to be "special," so she was going to stay home and organize everything.

Suddenly, she was in the kitchen and living room, going back and forth giving Lucille instructions, thwarting the celebration she had planned. I heard Lucille mutter, "I ain't botherin with you." But my mother had the last word, throwing into the garbage all Lucille's food: fried chicken, mashed potatoes, even the cornbread and the birthday cake that was lemon meringue pie topped with strawberries.

She made sure there was nothing sweet about my turning 16.

My mother continued to glare at me and indulge her rites of wantonness, and her admiration for stories of sensational sex and extravagant women grew. By then, my life crammed full of too many contradictory things, I would imitate the bruising physicality of Wilson Pickett, shouting "I'm a midnight mover," while I longed for a love so great that I had to destroy it, all the while seducing all comers in the name of romance. Whichever role I took on, I would be doomed, since everyone knew that enchantment dies. Any glamour or love was eclipsed by foreboding. Anything besides glamour or love was futile digression. Nothing beautiful could last, ever, and the glitter of beauty was never anything more than presumption anyway, the illusion that I could recover something sweet from everything I should have banished.

Just Close Your Eyes

I CAN LIVE THROUGH it again, the sense of something on my cheek early one morning in the late, late summer. In the mirror the thing looks like a beauty mark, dark and round. Only later, driving my car down West End Avenue and stopped in the traffic that has beset Nashville since the *New York Times* named it the "It City," I see that it's a tick, smaller than another one that had hung off my back or the one embedded in my waist until just a few days ago. Doctors identified the new tick, unlike the other two specimens, as a Rocky Mountain, though one of them disagreed, claiming it was a Brown Dog tick.

The ticks come to me while I sleep in my house. They have not taken to my dog, just me. What is this place to which I came with such abandon?

Native Americans of the Cherokee, Chickasaw, and Shawnee tribes hunted in the area around Nashville before the first white settlers arrived in the early 18th century. A friend who lived across town told me not long after I arrived that the Indians never wanted to settle here. "They wouldn't even sleep overnight," he said. They didn't like it, since the city lies so low in a dell that no air can escape. Instead, air settles "soft like syrup" into this basin of a city, poisoning everything inside.

I am tangled up in greed and the rot of pride, lured to Vanderbilt with a high salary and an endowed chair named for Robert Penn Warren, the poet, novelist, and literary critic who, underappreciated and fired from Vanderbilt, ended up at Yale. He wrote a stunning book that few people have heard of, lost as it was in the success of *All the King's Men*. Published in 1943 — just a year after my parents left Nashville for Atlanta — *At Heaven's Gate* is the true story of the Southern investment and banking empire Caldwell & Company, called Murdock and Company in the novel. Its development schemes and investment concerns wiped out homes, routed families, dispossessed farmers, and despoiled the environment for financial gain. Setting his novel in Nashville during the banking panic and crash of 1929-1932, Warren indicted the political graft and voracious cruelty of the burgeoning South. But he also created Sue Murdock. A cross between Scarlett O'Hara, Phèdre, and Emma Bovary, she remains one of the great, unrecognized women characters in fiction. Carrying the weight of the novel in her bones, in the slant of her hip, in the cheek of her challenge to the world around her, she kowtows to no one and dies a sordid death in the world of men.

I just found a note I wrote on the inside front leaf of Joseph Blotner's biography of Robert Penn Warren that reminded me of the dream I thought I had begun to live when I moved back to Nashville. "The magnolia smell, so long awaited, comes into the porch. At last, the blooms are coming to the lower branches. I pick them and put them to float in a bowl in my kitchen. Now, finally, I have a chance to do what had never been possible in my childhood, for there is no mother now, and all is glory and possibility. I thank God for this chance."

How deluded I was. It didn't take long for things to turn bad. There's no such thing as chance. My mother came back, bringing her lush and vanishing world along with her. A Calvinist by instinct, I know that everything is written in the good book anyway, pre-ordained and tailor-made for me, damned from the start. Like my mother, I am trapped by the hurt and harm hiding behind the genial romance of the South. But worse still, I know that I will never be free of the past, that it will never quit feeding on the present.

After my mother died, I learned that she and my father lived on Carden Avenue, just two blocks away from where I live now. My cousin Jean told me during an early morning phone call that my parents rented a house on the same block where she spent her childhood, when "Uncle Sam," her father and my father's older brother, moved the family from Brooklyn to Nashville. I never knew that my parents lived here. But I somehow sensed my mother striding alongside me, still giddy from her travels in Mexico, just as was in the early '40s, gliding, I imagine, with extraordinary ease. How did I think I could ever leave her?

When my father brought his young bride to the South, he wasn't working. He must have been some kind of genius to achieve so much after the hard knocks of his childhood. With his three brothers and one sister, he came from Aleppo, Syria, traveling in steerage, and he recalled his delight in drinking milk ladled out of huge troughs on board the ship. They landed at Ellis Island and joined their parents on Delancey Street, near Seward Park on New York's Lower East Side. They arrived in time for the great flu pandemic in 1918. He was a teenager when his parents died from it. He told me stories about young Jewish gangsters, who took him and his brothers under their wing and gave them protection.

I kept only one book from my father's bookshelves after he died, Herbert Asbury's *The Gangs of New York: An Informal History of the Underworld*. Published in 1928, it tells the stories of early gangs, police, the war of the Tongs, the "dead rabbits riot," along with detail Ωed descriptions of Chinatown, Hudson Street, and the Lower East Side. I remember my father's lament for the deaths by electric chair at Sing Sing of his favorite gangsters: Gyp the Blood (formerly Harry Horowitz) and Lefty Louie (Louis Rosenberg), along with the gunmen Dago Frank and Whitey Lewis. If Haiti remained my mother's lodestone, my father ached for a Bowery that crawled with drunks, lookouts, decoys, and ladies of pleasure. Every morning in the shower he belted out with a joy and abandon a song I never heard at any other time:

> The Bow'ry, the Bow'ry
> They say such things and they do strange things,
> Oh the Bow'ry! The Bow'ry!
> I'll never go there any more.

After working his way through college at John Jay, my father got a law degree at Brooklyn College and opened an office on Lower Broadway. I found a piece of engraved stationery with his name, followed by:

Counsellor At Law
32 Broadway
New York City

———

Bowling Green 9-6170-1-2

"Unlucky, so unlucky," that's what he always said, when he recounted how he started his practice just as the Depression began. He left the law and traveled to Europe, working at what he called "Import/Export." He started a business, "Atlas Importing Company," returned with a lot of money, and married my mother in Brooklyn.

He brought my mother to Nashville at the end of 1940. A town bit hard by the Depression, it was beginning to prosper again. The Grand Ole Opry — now the oldest continuous radio program in the United States — had just premiered on NBC radio. That year the Ryman Auditorium opened with the fiddler and singer Roy Acuff and his "Smoky Mountain Boys" performing. By the time my parents arrived, Nashville had lost some of its fame as the "Athens of the South" — with its universities and the full-scale replica of the Parthenon (the massive, plaster, gold-plated Athena came only several decades later) — and ceded that dubious glory to the lost loving and earthy truths of country music. It became known as "the hillbilly capital of the United States."

Most of the Nashville my mother knew is demolished. Buildings are torn down here as easily as flowers are pulled up before their time. "New flowers for new seasons," a neighbor explained, as she ripped them out of her yard. Virtually the only buildings remaining from my parents' days are the Parthenon and the Hermitage Hotel — named after Andrew Jackson's plantation just 10 miles east of downtown. Then it was known, somewhat more exotically, as Hotel Hermitage. In the late 1960s, Interstate

40 wiped out the great jazz and blues clubs on Jefferson Street, along with the African American communities that thrived there.

A glamorous lady of the South, that's what my father wanted. So he dressed my mother up and took her dancing at the Oak Bar and Grill Room of the Hotel Hermitage, where Francis Craig and his orchestra broadcast their music nationally on radio station WSM. I pass the marker at the house Craig lived in whenever I walk down my street. The young Tennessean Frances Rose Shore, who would later call herself Dinah Shore, used to perform at the bar. Her signature song "I'll Walk Alone" became the most popular song in America in 1944. "Till you're walking beside me, I'll walk alone." My father used to say she was "a sweet Jewish girl who made good."

My mother was never sweet. Nor was she very Jewish, since she always saw herself as a lapsed, not very spiritually-inclined Catholic. I still see her on Passover, as my father tried to conduct the Seder the way his father and grandfather (both rabbis) had done in Aleppo. She stood in the kitchen, talking on the telephone by the door of the dining room while my father read in a quick, muffled Sephardic chant. She just couldn't take seriously all that somber reckoning with a past she never understood and rituals that meant nothing to her.

Years later in Atlanta, while my mother partied with her friends, my father watched "The Dinah Shore Show," as if he might return to an earlier, better time, when he had just embarked on married life. "See the USA in your Chevrolet/America's the Greatest Land of All," she sang in a pink organza dress, introducing the new "Power Glide" model in 1953, when I was just three years old. Although Shore had left Nashville a couple of years before they arrived, my father spoke as if he knew her. When I was young and too scared to sleep, he sometimes came into my room and sang a few words from "Yes, My Darling

Daughter." An old Ukrainian folk tune, it became a hit when Dinah Shore sang it on Eddie Cantor's show the year my parents returned from their honeymoon.

"Whenever you're frightened, and you think someone comes to hurt you, just 'Tell him your heart belongs to Papa,'" my father crooned.

Something about their past and everything that was hidden waits for me in these streets, in the light rustle of dead leaves, or when rain falls, bringing worms out of the cracks in the pavement.

I live on a famous street where the people are friendly and the women are talented. There are also lots of dogs, bad-tempered little dogs. They're usually white. Sometimes I hear reports of a fox near the creek or an owl in a tree. Outside at night I used to see a possum in the backyard, looking at me in the dark with eyes that seemed like stars. Once I saw five of them skulking, eyes shining, inside a huge drain on the corner of my street.

It's also a street with history. Before my parents got here, the "Whitland Avenue Poets" met at James Marshall Frank's house. With a balcony on either side set back in the trees, it still stands; and unlike other houses that have been lost to enlarging and remodeling, it looks now exactly as it did in the '20s. The poets John Crow Ransom, Donald Davidson, Allen Tate, and Robert

Penn Warren, the youngest member of the group, soon became known as "The Fugitives." On the corner of the next block is the mansion Luke Lea bought, probably with the money he made from unscrupulous deals with Caldwell & Company. A monument to greed — and though few know it, it is also a reminder of Warren's testament to scandal in *At Heaven's Gate* — standing as if new, pristine white with red roofs. The plaque on the street in front marks the origins of what is now Nashville's only newspaper, *The Tennessean*, but says nothing about the financial ruin Lea brought down on Tennessee, nothing about his land grabbing and deception while governor. Not even that he was governor.

How easy it is to hide that history in the glamour of old wealth and new in a town where money matters, whether it's made by developers or by contractors of private prisons. A burly neighbor, now dead, once told me that Luke Lea haunted the neighborhood. "The whole darn place is haunted. Luke never really left," he said. He told me a story about how Lea died one night downtown, but his family didn't know until the next morning. That night he came in, hung up his rain coat, put down his umbrella, and walked up the stairs without saying hello to anyone. Then my neighbor turned, looked at me, and said: "He gave up the ghost all right, gave it right back to his folks."

My mother liked Dinah Shore's "I'll Walk Alone" as much as my father did. I heard it when she lay in her bed reading or waiting to be served by Lucille. It was a song for those times in the day when shutters were drawn and women of leisure took their rest, while the sun still burned outside.

> I'll always be near you wherever you are each night
> In every prayer

If you call I'll hear you, no matter how far
Just close your eyes and I'll be there

Please walk alone and send your love and your kisses to
guide me
Till you're walking beside me, I'll walk alone

I walk alone, Mother. I'm closing my eyes. I know she's here with me in this house, not far from her old street where women still gossip and music plays. She never mentioned Nashville to me, but I asked her to move here after her stroke in Atlanta. She had already begun to lose her bearings by the time dementia set in. She used to wander the streets, mumbling, "People look strange here," so I tried to bring her to Nashville. "No," she said. "I'm staying in my house." Her mind wandered, but she knew enough to warn me after I bought the house I offered to share with her: "You've made a big mistake." I didn't know yet that she had lived just two blocks away.

One day, after she had been unusually quiet, she laughed, bent down low, stared, shuffled and sang: "We'll carry him home to Dixie on the Wabash Cannonball." I had no idea what she meant, and I didn't care, not then. I was used to the strangely ominous musings that came at the end of her life, part of a sequence that included "Baby, it's cold outside," "I'm all for you, body and soul," and especially, "The Old Gray Mare."

My mother looked at me and sang, as if throwing a curse: "The old gray mare she ain't what she used to be. Ain't what she used to be. Ain't what she used to be." Old age had always been the thing to fear most. She tried to keep it at bay, pumping her palm under her chin, sleeping on her back so wrinkles couldn't set, putting the whites of eggs under her eyes. Everyone, she told me, would end up with loose jowls and cheeks caved in, bags under their eyes and a shuffle in their walk. No one could be young forever. And "no one," she whispered, "loves you when you're old and gray." She reminded me that no matter what we did, how we looked, what we wore, we would always be nothing more than bodies gone to rack and ruin.

I live through it all again, as if it was only yesterday. A few years after my arrival in Nashville, my house seemed to change before my eyes. Footsteps down the hall and the sound of doors shutting reminded me that ghosts, like maggots, need death in order to live. Whether grubs or ghosts, they feed and live because they know that nothing is ever so dead that it can't be ripe again. But only those who fear know the resilience of the dead.

Lowdown and isolated in Nashville, I feel a growing need to learn about my mother's life in the town I can't begin to like. Two years ago I came across a photograph of my mother sitting next to my father after dinner out in Nashville. I know exactly where it was. An appliance store now stands on the site at the intersection of Highway 100 and Harding. The photo sits inside a cover with the name and address: "Colonial Dinner Club. Located on Harding Road. Nashville, Tennessee." A sketch of a quaint, white, wooden structure also graces the cover: a one-story house with awnings on the windows and a sign on top, free-standing letters that say "COLONIAL"; and in smaller letters, painted on the roof, "Dinner Club." Then inside, a woman with pearls on her neck and dogwood flowers in her hair:

There she is. I recognize her firmly arched brows and slightly uncertain smile, her pose graced as always in those early years by her superb hair, almost wild in the luxuriance of its curls. A candle is lit on her left, Scotch and wine bottles and a canister of sugar not quite in the middle of the table. My father looks bored, satiated, whether with food or my mother, no matter. He's had a shot of whisky. His hand covers hers. In just a year or two, they've gone from the raw beauty and adventure of driving through Mexico to a dinner table in Nashville.

Now I live here, though after 12 years, I still don't know my way around. Such willed ignorance: everything I sense somehow passes through her and then comes back to me as my own experience, and I am waiting to learn my way around the Nashville of 1941. For how could a place with so many parks and pleasantly smiling, friendly people make me so unhappy? Trapped in this town as she was, I am seduced by her. I know what she knew. I feel how she felt.

"If you can't have her, then you can become her": that's what I used to hear from a close friend, whenever he described what it meant to be possessed by what you most desire but can't ever get. I always thought the words were oddly twisted, but now I understand. They describe how longing works in the flesh. It always leaves its mark. If such an emotion remains unrequited, it will take its revenge. It consumes and takes over my self, turning me into the woman I thought I wanted, the mother who possesses me at last.

Someone's in the Kitchen

LUCILLE TOLD ME NOT to come in the kitchen. In my young days when I wanted to watch her slice vegetables and pluck chickens, she warned: "This is no place for the likes of you. I'm telling you, standing next to me at this counter won't get you nowhere at all. As good as looking a blind cat in the eye. And you know you don't want to do that."

But I did. I wanted to see that blind cat all the way through, into her milky eyes and beyond. Sacred, that kitchen: the shiny surface near the sink covered in blood, the gizzards and neck put aside to be fried later and eaten — Lucille's special delicacy — and her tidying up after the mess of flour and butter, the thick batter where she rolled chicken breasts and thighs before frying them in the skillet at dinnertime for the "white folks." That's what she used to say, with a grin and a nod, adding: "But we get the good parts." Lucille and I ate in the den, watching television. Gunfights where white men duked it out at the corral and in the streets, while I imagined my mother out on the town with her lascivious ways, the smell of her perfume, and the whisky on her breath.

My mother stood on the porch with a drink. She grabbed me by my arm, pulled me into the house, and sang her favorite song. "You ain't seen nothin' yet/The best is yet to come and babe, won't it be fine?" Nothing was good enough for her, ever. Even the best meant the worst. "I'm gonna teach you to fly." Again, I see the yardman chasing my chickens with an ax. Chickens squawking on the bloodstained dirt, human eyes closed in rapture, the jewels my mother wore.

Even if Lucille told me not to watch her in the kitchen, she didn't mind when she looked around and saw me by her side. Anything could turn into a learning moment, what she called "studying." She wanted to put me right, get my "head turned on straight," since the South was "bad enough to hurt you too." Hate was in the eyes of the white men who were tall and proud. Hate caused fires to start, glass to break, guns to kill, clubs to hit, dogs to chase and bite. The dogs were big. They were German Shepherds not Blue Tick or Red Bone hounds. The eyes of the white men tracked me, and not just their eyes, their mouths too. They grinned as they beat up people kneeling in prayer. They smirked as they circled round reporters whose cameras they smashed.

Lucille and I stood in the kitchen. When my mother came home, she screamed at me, her polished nails and slender fingers clamped down on the scruff of my neck and the collar of my shirt as she dragged me away from Lucille and her cooking. I grew up sensing that the kitchen was off limits; the only time my mother looked at me with eyes that did not go hard and a touch that did not hurt was when I stood in our living room in front of a mirror dressed up like a trussed animal, uncomfortable and distressed. Never in the kitchen, and as a child I never saw my mother cook anything. Only later in her life, when I came home to visit, did I see her standing in the kitchen around midnight, feet bare and in her nightgown or robe, baking baklava and what her Ashkenazi friends called "mandelbrot." By then, she was alone in Atlanta. I watched her, adrift like a woman lost in time, chopping pistachios, rolling out dough on a floured board, back and forth, pulling and flattening it out until it was tissue-thin. In the large freezer downstairs, she piled up shoeboxes filled with desserts, stacked and set out on wax paper.

With most of her friends dead and my father gone — except when he hovered, as she used to tell me, up on the ceiling by the light in her bedroom — my mother remained alone. She seemed so out of character, no longer the woman of glamour, either out on the town or lying in bed. She had grown old, just like the house that was falling into ruin around her. Even before the final illness that ate away at her mind and memory, she lived in ever-intensifying reminders of what had been lost.

After she died, boxes of her clothes came to Nashville. Along with photos I had never seen, and these boxes full of clothes, came another box filled with silk underwear, bras, panties, and slips. As I removed this lingerie, I found a denim-covered, old-fashioned ring notebook, the kind I grew up using in elementary school. Of all the things recovered after my mother's death, nothing shocked me like this relic. It contains the gist of her life: a record of a spirit that lived without my recognition. On its cover, I see my writing. I must have been very young. The words strike me hard. I loved her to death. And this is the haunt, not dolls that I found in her basement with their heads torn off or the fur coats covered in mold just like skinned animals, cast off and forgotten. This is the book of her life. I wrote across the front of it:

Sophie	Edmond	Joan
Dayan	Dayan	Dayan

Or did my mother write these words? In the center of the cover is the word "Recipes," and then, further down: "Food: yum, yum." A grimoire, a book of spells that held the secret to her hopes, and it overwhelms me like nothing else that remained after she died. There are scribbles in pencil all over, along with, in very small letters fading now, words that look like a child's writing, copying what was already written out but now in a straight line: "Sophie Dayan Edmond Dayan," and then below them, faint, tiny, and without a last name: "Joanie."

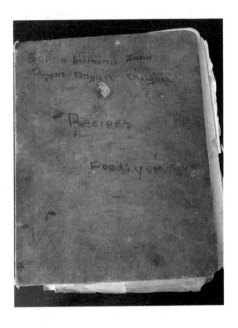

The notebook is filled with handwritten notes for all kinds of food, clippings of recipes or of photos — "Pig in Blanket," "Southern Fried Chicken," or "Red Noodles and Beef" — and lists of vegetables, with instructions about cooking things as simple as string beans. A testimonial to her reading, it was also the way she learned to speak English. "Savory meat balls." "Hattie's Steaks." "Onion and Pickle Sauce." I imagine her writing down these words onto the sheet of lined paper with three ring holes that lies in front of me on my desk.

> String beans
> Cut string beans and wash
> Pieces of veal muscles
> Pieces of bones
> Put meat on bottom of pan and string beans on top.
> Put in a little oil and cook on slow fire.

A witch's brew too simple not to be ritual. Is this a ritual of domestic life, or some kind of incantation, a litany of fortune in the lineaments of beans, muscles, and bones?

In the same box, I also found two spiral notebooks, with double pocket dividers stuffed with clippings. Each notebook had slick yellow covers and 152 sheets of wide-ruled paper, three quarters of the pages covered in her handwriting. They reveal someone I never knew. Not a cold beauty, the lady who never lifted a finger, or the half-awake woman who rang a bell for Lucille in the morning and drank herself silly with friends at night. This is a younger woman, buoyant in anticipation. One clipping, quite worn, describes how to make hamburgers, and in the pages of her writing, I came across a page that reads as if a story about a place called "Hamburg," and a character named "Ham Burg" — who gets "browned in hot fat in skillet," or "Hamburg bean pot," with salt and pepper. Young and just married, she seems to believe that if she could just make those beans or get that hamburger right, all would be well. She set about shaping herself into that thing called "wife," a Southern wife, who tried to realize her identity through her persistence in the kitchen. Amassing recipes and notes and magical thinking. Nothing is Haitian, nothing that resembled what she might have eaten growing up in Port-au-Prince, although there were a couple Syrian dishes crowded out by everything American. In these scrambled newspaper and magazine clippings, I see how my mother willed herself to be a housewife.

My mother was never sincere. How could she be? My father had turned her into a mannequin of his heart's desire. He lured her away from a past that taught her independence. He foreclosed her fantasies of the future. But she cooked. That she loved — before I came into her life, she cooked, to win my father's love; and long after that, when she was much older, she baked, to remember him. What lay in between, the parties and the lust, the laughter and the dirt, was all I had ever known as a girl, all that obsessed me.

One photo remains from the unknown land of kitchen days — she stands, a young bride, in what I bet is Nashville, with her hair pulled back in a style that I never knew, holding a shish kebab, her face serene and grave in the glare of the window. My mother took herself seriously then. She had the chance to matter.

Blood is on the kitchen ceiling. The red flecks appeared about a year ago. I knew my mother wouldn't stay long under the ground.

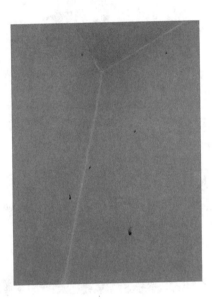

Thomas, our yardman when I was a girl, described the dead who come back as not being able to stay still. "They'll be looking at you like they're in the movies. That's the way they come out. They don't come on real. They come out like a show or something. Sometimes, they come back like steam going over you. And that steam's going to be the ghost. They don't come out natural. That's why it hurts so bad."

But my mother comes back with a fleshly message from above, a trail of blood. No steam or shadow for her.

"Nobody's going to cook in this kitchen but me," I hear my mother telling me, now that she has found her bearings in my Tudor house with a magnolia out front and a dogwood tree and pink and white azaleas just as I remembered them from our backyard in Atlanta. My friends can't understand how I stay in the house, and I admit I'm hard put to explain it. Why don't windows shutting and feet walking "scare the living daylights out of me," as Lucille used to say? The funeral trains keep coming down the tracks, along with the cries of orphans in the night. I hear them: the whistle blows. "I hear the train a' comin'/It's rolling round the bend/And I ain't seen the sunshine since I don't know when."

Johnny Cash is here, along with Lucille, Thomas, my mother, and all the other spirits that live in the heavy blowing trees and the rank smelling flowers. It's a good crowd. I'm never lonely, and I'm glad my father won't have anything to do with all of us, since his heroes of suffering — Jeremiah and Spinoza — sure would put a damper on things.

My friend Freddie had been hit by a train walking across the tracks early one morning. Thomas warned me I wouldn't want to see him. "He'll just stand there looking like a post, and he won't say nothing. It'll scare you. You'll go into spasms." I kept asking him how I could see Freddie again. Thomas said that Freddie would return with the suit he was buried in not quite tacked on him. It would not fit him. He repeated what he always told me when we spoke about raising the dead. "You don't want to see no one you can't touch, do you? See someone you talk to, and they don't answer, do you?" Because I felt so strongly that it was Freddie I wanted to see, I was told, "That's why you won't see him."

One day after I'd been out of Nashville and away from home for a month or so, I walked in the kitchen and saw maggots on the stove. They squirmed. As soon as I sponged them off, more fell. Something had died, I thought, up in the attic, becoming food for maggots. Lyle Brim, the "wildlife removal" man, climbed a ladder, removed one of the light fixtures and shined his flashlight up into the opening. "You can't have maggots without a host," he said. "These are maggots, but there's no flesh for them to feed on." He sawed about so much round the hole that insulation came down, along with more maggots. "It's like poltergeists," he mumbled, as he watched some falling, others diving onto gas burners on the range. "It stinks like hell, even if it ain't nothing up there," he concluded. But I knew there was.

I knew that my mother wanted me to see her, but I tried not to. When I heard a window slam unaccountably in the far study, heard footsteps, or saw new sprinklings of blood that suddenly appeared on another kitchen cabinet, I said out loud: "Okay, I love you" and thought to myself how attached I was becoming to this house, a house that had become her special place.

At night when it's dark and I'm alone, I fear someone real and big breaking in through a window. But when it comes to my mother, I feel not just dread, but longing. I know she's here. She comes in many forms, but her breath is always upon me. I touch my neck so that I can shut out the sense of her hand, tapping on my skin.

> Someone's in the kitchen with Dinah
> Someone's in the kitchen I know
> Someone's in the kitchen with Dinah
> Strummin' on the old banjo!

"Now don't you tell me you can't hear me tell you about that railroad," Lucille said one night in Atlanta. "You better hide like a snake in the grass, if you don't want to fall under the ghost whip. Death's little black train is coming." But I also heard the laughter of white friends, as we sang "I've Been Working on the Railroad" on the way to camp up in the mountains of Asheville, North Carolina. We hooted and hollered, yelling out the words: "Dinah, won't you blow…/ Dinah won't you blow…/Dinah won't you blow your horn?" I smile now when I remember how the boys used to get nasty, and look girls in the eyes while they pursed their lips like they were going to blow on a trumpet. But we knew what they meant.

When it came to "Someone's in the kitchen with Dinah," Lucille had no truck with sex or the high romance that masked it. "You know as sure as the day is long how much she suffered, pulled at and ripped into by the man." The lash in the prison camps, that she knew, too, and the splintered wood of the tracks; and over it all, the white man on horseback in the broad-brimmed hat with a shotgun slung over his shoulder. Sensing this real and present memory, she was steeped in her bones with the bad history of the South. Only whites could rollick with that song, thinking about a woman named Dinah, who might or might not be a black woman, who might be free or maybe still a slave.

Lucille made sure I understood how blood mixed with dirt when the violence came. As late as the 1960s, I saw black men, shackled at the ankles, linked together by chains, and dressed in what we knew as "zebra stripes," working their time along the highways of Fulton County. My father told me not to look at the men chained up, but he told me that his favorite actor was

Paul Muni whose performance in "I Am a Fugitive from a Chain Gang" changed his life.

Everything that mattered to me came from Lucille — she made me see what my parents hoped I would disregard. She took me by the arm and said: "Don't you ever not pay attention to those men who walk in chains." But I didn't know that until later, until I felt how ghosts kept step with me here in Nashville, standing in the kitchen where maggots make their home.

Lucille taught me how convicts were leased out to work on the railroads, in the mines, and even in the fields. Standing next to her while she concentrated on her job at the stove, I learned how the police were known as "the laws." I grew up hearing about "meat that takes directions from someone." She threw raw steak on the skillet and told me about the paterollers who would get me if I walked outdoors in the dark. "With their white cone hoods and their white capes," they'll come at you like "ghosts in the night."

I grew up in that kitchen. I learned why my mother didn't want me there. Ostensibly white and graced with laughter, she didn't want me to be where "the help" was supposed to be. But since she never stayed home, Lucille and I shared stories of intimacy and threat. "It comes on like a flash of white in the darkness to steal your soul and thieve your mind, but it feels so good," Lucille warned. Then she sang, "I ain't got long to stay here, I'm just gonna steal away."

> Fie, fi, fiddly i o
> Fie, fi, fiddly i o
> Fie, fi, fiddly i o
> Strumming on the old banjo

Nothing is lost, mother. What you left behind when you married my father comes back through me in ways you would never have liked. But I like to think my undone hair, un-manicured nails and elephant-tough feet, along with books and politics — everything you despised — have sown the soil for your return. You come back with mango juice on your hands, your feet naked on the floor, all the feeling you held back and sweetness you destroyed as you got the knack of a life that would only hurt you.

At Home on the Other Side

LUCILLE. Lucille. Hold me tight like you used to. I'm calling out to you just as I did when you put me to bed, turned off the lights, and headed down the hall to the den where you slept on the sofa. Those were the only nights when I was genuinely un-afraid, no matter how many scary stories you told. I was never alone as long as you were there with the hair net drawn tight over your head covered in pomade to loosen the curls. You are everywhere still, in sight of a full moon or with the crack of light under my bedroom door; and as I grow older, I see you at the bottom of the stairs to the basement, just as you stood when I was little, making sure I didn't follow you. Bending down low with your hands on your hips, you sang about the chariot of the Lord: "rockin', Lord, rockin', Lord, calm and easy, I got a home on the other side." Fierce in your body, you taught me how to think out of the goodness of your heart.

Though I didn't understand then what I know now, I was caressed into a quality of imagination that stirs my blood, even as I'm filled with regret for what I've lost. When my father took our picture, I fell back into the crease of your arm and leaned in so close that my head found the softness of your cheek. Our two right eyebrows are both arched exactly alike. My eyes look sleepy and slightly skewed, but yours look out so directly that in staring back at you now my heart skips a beat.

Given the wayward ethics of my house, the demands on me to be pretty and sweet always seemed strange. You tempered that pretension by allowing me, as long as my parents weren't around, to jump up and down on my bed, dressed in a slip and wearing a dog tag. I was about seven or eight years old. Where you got that metal necklace or when you had it made, I don't know; but I kept it for a long time. On it was my name and address. You always told me that if I got killed by someone or just passed away peacefully in the night, no matter where I was, people would know how to find me and get me home. You let me drag my mattress off my bed, hang washrags on the windows, and keep all kinds of bugs in jars on the sills. I played with frogs and hung out with boys down the street, pretending to be a hobo, decked out in britches with holes and shirts without sleeves.

You sewed patches over the holes. You gave me the chance not to live a lie. I am isolated now without you, and it never occurred to me to wonder about my true origins. No matter how my mother dressed me up or my father bound me to his idea of morality, over the roads and across fields I ran, climbing hills, and orphaned into your arms I rode on the backs of trains, moving no matter how sad or afraid through the darkness until I got to the light.

Not far from Lexington Avenue, on the Upper East Side of New York, you returned to me late one night while I was in Michael's Pub. A small place, filled with smoke and lots of drinking, it was just the kind of place you would have liked. It was 1987. Of all the places for you to manifest your love. Maybe it was the tables and chairs, all so close together, the whitish-brown walls, the dim light or the clatter of glasses filled with whisky; but most likely it was the music. You had been dead over a dozen years, yet it was as if you were again sitting close to me on the sofa in Atlanta. Not an apparition, but instead in the gloom of this unfamiliar room, you stood next to me with an odd stiffness and gazed at me, or rather, looked right through me.

Freddie Moore was performing. "Fred on the washboard," the ad announced. In the midst of well-heeled whites and seated close to my clever date — once a Yale graduate student in Russian and now an oil man with a deep intelligence about the best vintages of Pauillac — I kept my eyes on Moore, though it struck me that you had taken my hand. We both listened to his voice, singing low, and I felt your arms around me. When someone asked me, "How's your fettuccine?" I was already gone, dying into the past where I could live again, caught up in your strength, just like that day when I tumbled all the way down that hill in Atlanta, landing hard in the dirt. you came over to me and muttered, "That hill done knocked the breath out of you." Then you whispered intently, "I got my thrill on Blueberry Hill."

A couple hours later, when I returned alone to my apartment after the pub, I wrote a page of notes. I read them now and feel, again, your death and know that though you are gone from the life, you remain inside me, just like an embryo that grows, taking on fuller shape with each passing day. "She is the answer to my life. Not my natural mother, but Lucille who demanded more than I could ever give." My longing for you changed what might have been mere lament. Yes, you, too, if I couldn't have you, then I wanted to become you. I now lived a life that was as far away from you as ever, in New York, where there was no way I could get close to the snakes, spiders, and lizards we loved. I had strayed far from the dandelion flowers with their white and fluffy heads of seeds that we blew on so that they scattered everywhere like feathers. I remembered Moore's words and wrote them down too; he sang, "so thin, so cool and fair." His "wild man blues" seemed to speak to me, telling me to release you: "Let her go, let her go, god bless her." But I am quite unable to let you go. I once tried calling the number you gave me after I moved to New York. It was disconnected. You used to ask me: "When are you bringing me up there to take care of everything, honey?" I failed you, I know. But I'm listening hard for you. I hear you call my name, and I see the flame of your lighter. "Ya, ya, ya."

An entire history of strength and talent soaring high on the current of racism and struggle: though you seemed to acquiesce in my parents' wishes, laboring long to turn out my long curls and dressing me in lace dresses, you took me into another world. When you got angry at something I'd done — when I laughed at how you read to me, refused to eat my dinner, or threw a tantrum — you punished me by locking me out of the den. When my parents were out of town, you left me alone, after telling me how people said I was "crazy." You always repeated, "They was talking about you on the bus."

You scared "the daylights out of me," just like you warned you would; and Lord knows how you crammed my mind full of ghosts, in and out of their skin, hiding under my bed, squatting outside my windows, or haunting that special train you called "Yellow Dog." I never knew what you meant until after you were gone. I always imagined a yellow dog with red eyes running along the tracks. But I bet you were letting me know about the train Bessie Smith made famous when she sang W.C. Handy's "The Yellow Dog Blues." "Oh, listen," you whispered, "You can hear that moaning." With shoulders thrust forward and stooping low down, you hummed a song about how the Southern Railway met the Yazoo Delta. It was, I later learned, acquired by the Yazoo and Mississippi Valley Railroad and known as "The Dog" or the Yellow Dog:

> I'm goin' where the Southern cross the Yellow Dog.
> I'm goin' where the Southern cross the Yellow Dog.

"Cross my heart and hope to die," I used to repeat after you. I made the sign of the cross and lay down next to you, afraid but also longing for the shadow of death to possess me, as long as dogs howled and trains whistled.

My mother was never home and couldn't be bothered to take me to school or pick me up, nor did she attend PTA meetings. You were the one. My friends and I all waited for you to arrive in your green Deluxe Bel Air Chevrolet with the cushions piled high on the front seats, along with plaid slipcovers that hid tears in the leather. As far as I can tell now from pictures, it must have been a 1950 model, just about my age. Since you didn't want me walking anywhere alone, I got to know that car well, its strong smell of what must have been sandalwood and its warmth in both winter and summer. I rode in your car until junior high, when you taught me how to drive and I got my "learner's license," which meant I could drive at 15 as long as you were sitting next to me. Years later, Thomas reminded me that you acted like I was a "caged doll": "She kept you tight. Wouldn't let you out of her sight. You'd be in that carriage or on your feet, it didn't matter, 'cause she wouldn't let you out."

Your car was never just a vehicle to get around in. It called me to another place. We could be going to school but at the same time we might just be heading out of this broken road of sorrow and into the real home somewhere beyond. When you used to sing "Swing Low Sweet Chariot," I thought you meant that your car, pitching round the curve, was also the chariot that crossed over to the other side. The chariot didn't swing low, no matter what the words said. It moved horizontally with wheels upon wheels borne out over the dust and rolling calm and easy over bumps along the way. "If you get there before I do," you turned to me and smiled, "tell all my friends I'll be coming there too, coming for to carry me home."

"Well, well, well. Well, well, well." I know you're up in glory with the chariots of fire, God's throne, and all the bones gathering nearby. "Dem bones dem bones gonna walk around. Now hear the word of the Lord." You and I used to talk a lot about the sea of disjoined bones that once reconnected into skeletons actually come to life. You explained how "they don't bloom like grass, cause they're dried up, dead, and buried, clean cut off," but "no matter how dry, they goin' to rise again." Then you told me to come outside, and once we were on the patio, you stretched out your arms, and declared, "as sure as the wind blows, honey, you know these bones will rise."

> Ah, well, de toe bone connected wid de foot bone,
> De foot bone connected wid de anklebone,
> De ankle bone connected wid de leg bone,
> De leg bone connected wid de knee bone,
> De knee bone connected wid de thighbone,
> Rise an' hear de word of de Lord!

You slumped down, touched your feet, then jumped up and landed hard on the pavement. Standing stark straight in the sun, with music and brightness all around, you showed me how everyone will be up and proud, all "dem bones" come together again.

Lucille always protected my mother, covering up her wandering ways and cursing me to the devil as a "busybody," but I doubted my mother's loyalty to her. She wasn't jealous of what Lucille and

I shared — she never reckoned with the magic of early summer at the creek or gave a damn for the sight of a lightning bug. She had been socialized into the artifice of charm and glamour that came with life in the South and lost herself. She became the jaded observer of her own traits, her mouth frozen, always posing, manacled by the glitter all around her. She summoned Lucille with curt demands, ringing the bell every morning.

My mother's indifference dismantled my life. Lucille, dead animals, flowers, trees, and insects, the words from songs are in all the places where memories of myself might have begun to give shape to my life. Out of the dust and confusion of my childhood, only the desire to escape emerges. I hated the South. From the age of five, I kept a suitcase packed under my bed, ready to run when I could. When I was 13, my father decided I wasn't fit to eat dinner with them. He came home from work one night, and I asked him whether he would close his store and join the protestors on the street. He told me he'd "stop me thinking such dangerous thoughts," and I yelled that he was nothing but a racist, even though I knew that compared to other whites at that time, he was one of the moderates who embraced an "Atlanta too busy to hate," and believed in a gradual, "reasonable" approach to integration. He told me I was headed for an unhappy life, and my mother — not to be outdone in forecasting my inevitable doom — said yet again: "You'll be left holding the bag." But it was Lucille's words that stayed with me always. She wanted nothing to do with talk about race-hating intolerance or black pride: "That girl's brains been filled with demons. She's gone crazy."

A photo of my mother and me from five years earlier captures the lush green, the dogwoods and azaleas of spring. My mother and I are standing on the flagstone path winding in front of our house in Fulton County, in northeast Atlanta. My mother must be 36, and I'm eight. We look uncomfortable, caught in a pose that tries to appear natural when everything about it is strained. Even my mother's feet in their open-toed heels look cramped, with the big toe bent over its neighbor. Looking up from her feet, however, a lightness takes shape, as my eye follows her legs, taut and lean under her tight skirt, up to the hip casually slung, to the right arm, with bangles on the wrist and a cigarette held loosely in her hand. But the eyes are strained, too much of the eyebrow is plucked, and the face, though beautiful, looks dead, the smile held too long.

What a beauty! Everyone used to say. And she was gorgeous, whether posing for my father, dressing for the club, playing tennis, or talking on the phone. Everything I write about her, the woman I never knew, sounds like a cliché. In the photo, next to her. My left foot is pointed. An aspiring ballerina, I'm wearing a tutu, but have nothing of what my teacher Miss Merilee called "grace." On my head, with my hair tightly pulled back, someone has put a metal crown covered with glitter. One of my arms creeps up my mother's back, reaching up only to the armpit, and the other held away by my mother's left hand. Her grasp on my wrist does something strange: my hand is crooked, my fingers disconnected and limp. There is no life in them. My eyes seem dim, as if I am unable to focus, my sense of the world a blur.

But things became definite and sharp when I walked outside with Lucille or sat across the table from her. She brought snakes into my life. There were "black snakes," "garter snakes," "king snakes," and "rattlers," but her favorite one, the one I can't stop thinking about, was the "cottonmouth," her beloved "water moccasin." Not only was it venomous, but it also did something peculiar with its mouth that she especially liked. "Don't you ever look inside of a moccasin's mouth," she warned me. That meant that she was eager for me to do just that. Whatever was forbidden, we went after. And there was nothing stranger than if you dared to look through the snake's open mouth into something so white and pure that it looked like a cotton ball. A gaping beauty, that's what it was, the open-mouthed snake with eyes like a dog's. Lucille described its skin as "smooth as a baby's fur," but I always remembered its bright colors, banded brown or yellow or black, looking like that "coat of many colors" I learned about in Sunday school. So anytime we saw a cottonmouth, we squatted to get a closer look, and Lucille called out the names Jacob and Esau. "They always fighting," she said. "Meaner than two spotted skunks in the holler."

Though most people suppose that a "cottonmouth" is different from a "water moccasin," Lucille knew better. They were "cottonmouth water moccasins" to her. Late at night she walked alone, revisiting our hikes from the day before; and the next morning she told me: "That snake we saw, it ain't nothing but your water mama, thick as the trunk of a tree with a head like a Pit Bull and jowls like tits." Don't threaten it, and it won't bite. And stay away from "them breeding balls down by the creek." Oh, those snakes were happy. I recall how they swam in the water or basked in the sun on the earthy banks, sometimes with their tail hidden by leaves.

When I got to Haiti for the first time at 19, I was told by a taxi driver that my *met-tet,* the "master of my head" or *lwa* that protected me and became my god, was Danbala: the Haitian serpent god that keeps the sky from falling to the earth. Always represented with his partner Ayida wedo, he is one of the oldest gods, originating in Dahomey but reinvigorated on the soil of Saint Domingue when the Africans who served him became slaves in the New World.

A tough spirit with huge reserves of jealousy, he watches over me. I serve him with rum, black coffee, and the white of an egg resting in a bowl of flour. And I sing in Creole, while lighting candles, "Papa Danbala, mesi. Mesi, Papa Danbala. Thank you, Papa Danbala. Oh, snake of the waters. Look for Danbala, who dives down deep. Oh Danbala wedo, you plunge to the bottom of the waters." He's in my blood, just like Lucille who lives on as my ancestor spirit. Some say he is insatiable and greedy, but I know him as patient. He forgives me when I travel and he misses out on morning coffee or when I leave for months at a time and take him with me, far away from his altar. I know that when the time comes, I will descend like him into the waters on the long road to Guinea. Lucille awaits me there.

Get Down

"I'LL SEE YOU in a little bit," the man in the truck said. I had no idea what he meant, since I didn't know him. He looked like the kind of person my parents warned me not to talk to. Someone from out in the country, he was very white with eyes that looked through me. But Lucille didn't mind my meeting people she called "white crackers with cooties in their hair." She figured I was in the enviable position of being not too white or too black, which meant that I could find out more things about such people than she could. That's how we lived: she told me secrets about how to win the fight and sent me out into the world not exactly like bait, but pretty close to it, like an expendable spy. We waited. Waited until I got old enough to be mostly on my own, and by that time, as she knew, I'd have learned my lesson about which kind of people to fear, when to hate, and when to brawl.

We lived in a gangster movie of her making, where a simple walk down the street might be the chance for another showdown or a duck behind bushes to hide from the bad guys or the police. There was no time for sentiment or romance. I learned that only the privileged and pasty-faced spent their days with such foolishness. Our neighborhood held wonders that others didn't notice. Not just all kinds of insects, snakes, spiders, possums, June bugs, and ground squirrels, but also what she named the "Wandering Dead." Sometimes they hid under the dirt or came out in the bodies of rats or dogs. The men with grins and cold eyes, however, were what I had to look out for.

So, when I saw the man in the truck pulling up alongside me, I stared at him long enough for him to ask whether I wanted to take a ride. "You want to come on up here?" he asked. I said, "No," but I knew I couldn't run because I was supposed to stand still right where I was. That was the only way. Only when he opened the door did I decide to run. Lucille told me I'd done the right thing, since I didn't have anything to fight with. Another time, I was walking down the street with my friend Peggy Ellen when a white man in a sedan stopped and asked us to come for a ride. I ran so fast that Peggy got real mad when we got back to my house, saying that it was like the time I ate all the chocolate chip cookies without offering her a bite. "You're just a selfish thing," she shouted, and swore that she'd never walk with me again. She kept her word. When I told Lucille I had lost my best friend, and the other girls had stopped talking to me too, she told me not to worry, since they were "Tom Fool whites and never liked you anyway."

Now that I've returned to the South, an old fear beckons. That's why Lucille keeps coming back to me. The white men are still tall and proud and their eyes bold and fearless. But I am not scared anymore. Because I walk with Stella, my American Staffordshire who is always recognized as a Pit Bull, I can go down the street and look straight into their eyes when they stare at me from their trucks. Their smiles make me feel good. Their gaze takes me to a place of comfort that I don't understand. Something that gives me a respite from sensing that I don't belong, that I am not right in my skin.

What that something is I do not know. But I have a hunch that it has a lot to do with terror. They still do not like me. I know it. Their friendliness, like my nonchalance, puts us both at the edge of what is permissible. We are both faking it. Terror is always like that. It skirts the real. It looks to the past. Our talk carries the old scorn in its pauses. I like that I get to pretend politeness and live again the fright of growing up, when dogs and big white men with guns were patrolling the streets and talking on the television news. I was as afraid of my mother's disdain as of the violence of the white men who kicked and spat at black demonstrators two blocks from my father's store. But I was not part of that struggle either. I belonged nowhere.

Now, 50 years later, when I see white men looking at my dog and me, I quicken in sight of their smiles. Are they grinning because they like the breed? Inviting me to bond with them in having a game dog, a dog that knows no fear and never gives up, as loyal as the day is long? Or is it that same old lethal grin, telling me with their eyes and in the twist of their lips that I might be walking now but they could hobble me anytime they wanted. Not only could they kill. They toyed with, tortured, and trashed. And they're feeling real good nowadays, since hate has returned in the time of Trump, but with the spark of celebrity and patina of luxury. They're all rallying around money mongers like "flies to shit," as Lucille said. These "poor whites, they don't never go away," she said. They kept to themselves and sometimes, if you happened to take a trip out into the countryside, you might come across them. They were always waiting. Just like in *Easy Rider* or *Deliverance*, perhaps, but also on any street in Birmingham, the highways of Georgia, the churches of Mississippi, or anywhere else where white domination mattered more than life. They waited in a grocery store, behind any lunch counter, any place where ordinary services were offered. As I said, my mother was always sensitive to white women, especially when they worked in stores. Until old age she would talk back and say things like: "Don't you look at me like that" or "What's wrong with you?" She saw through their friendliness. She hated their smiles. She knew that's when you had to be especially careful.

Thinking now about Lucille and my mother and their different reactions to "regular white people," I imagine that the whole problem had to do with sweetness. The very charm of the South, its much-touted hospitality, was something you had to crawl underneath in order to know the evil that lies hidden. "Know the dirt," Lucille used to say, "and you'll live a long life." And my mother relished a fight. They might despise her, but she would show them that she, too, could hate. I realize now that this "they" always happened to be white women: it didn't matter whether they were rich or poor, working in a store or attending the symphony.

With these women, her tightly controlled façade of whiteness never really worked, and she knew it. Her longing to be accepted was a failed enterprise, and she lashed out at those really white folks who treated her as if there was something wrong about her with their raw looks. "Who do they think they are," she asked, "acting like I don't belong here?" Lucille ignored whoever insulted her or whatever she didn't trust — going silent and striking her face of stone — but my mother became enraged, drew herself up tight, and said, as if she were spitting out, "Why are you looking at me like that?" Sometimes she mocked them, repeating their words with a high-pitched Southern accent, a kind of singsong voice. The encounter ended with their bafflement and my mother energized, outraged.

I knew the rage, along with the longing, of my mother; the hate of white men, the trickery of white women — all facades I learned to shy away from — resting whole and happy only in Lucille's thoughtfulness and ingenuity. When I was in graduate school, a man friend of mine came down to visit me in Atlanta. We drove to my favorite place, Fontana Village in the Smoky Mountains of North Carolina. I'm not sure why I liked going there so much during college and later, but I suppose it was because there I would see white folks square dancing, playing the music I loved to hear, though where I had ever heard it before I don't know.

My friend, a former Faulkner professor, with blond hair and blue eyes, and I rented a rowboat on the big lake. In the beauty of all that deeply wooded green, when we reached the other side of the lake, my friend had trouble turning the boat around. Something happened so that we sat there stalled, with him struggling mightily to get us going again. A man appeared on the bank and shouted: "You darn, sweating Yankee, why don't you get on back where you belong," or something close to it. Looking at me, he added, "What is a gal like you doing with a punk like that?" Then he rowed out to us, told my friend to watch while he turned us around and set the boat out in the direction of the dock.

Fiddlers and crooners abounded up there in the mountains of North Carolina. I found a thrill in these white lives so excited by the stomping of feet, the gasp of a good laugh and the lure of courtship. Only now do I know what it means to be held by a past that can be captured, all of it, in just a few words. Late in life I know that a song like "The Old Gray Mare" holds some kind of key to what really matters. Transfixed but unable to know exactly why, I am never free of its grip.

The old gray mare,
She ain't what she used to be
Many long years ago.

Oh mother, I'm talking to you now. How casually we take sheer beauty and grind it into the dirt. Your liveliness and gorgeous self, both deteriorated like the gray that began at the roots of your hair. I see you now with your eyes failing and your body closing down. Even then, you insisted that color be put on your hair. It was such a strange sight to see how patiently and serenely you sat in bed waiting for the dye to be applied by your caretaker — a woman named Jamie who, we learned later, used to strap your arms to the bed. By then, you were back in Brooklyn, far away from Georgia.

That's why I don't leave. No matter what happened to you here, it was never as bad as what awaited you up North. Lucille created a world that strengthened us as long as we were in the South with her. As long as she lived, we were blessed. We had wings, but if we wanted, we could just as easily dig deep into the earth. Giving us the full and perfect sound of her voice, she tried to keep us safe from harm as long as she lived. "Nothing bad can keep you down," she said, "if you know what you love." One way or the other, wherever I stand, I'm still heading toward her. No matter how old I am, everything that is in me still moves to her breath. She saved me from my mother's self-hate. Without her, I would be left with nothing but the fright of words whispered, fragments of an afternoon, bits about deceit, blood, and waste.

In a t-shirt sitting in the tub with a young girl, I was baptized into Christ. I was in my late thirties. The pastor prayed over me as he helped me duck my head in the water. Whether in or out of the water, I heard the prayers of the people, and knew how much I needed them, living under what I felt was my mother's curse. I was never freed from demons. I could never escape from the deep lying shadows that hovered in any room I inhabited. But in church, I lived again in song. I felt the Lord coming into my heart. The light came through the windows of the church that Reverend McDowell called "The Love Shack." "Wade in the water," he intoned. "Wade in the water, children." I was out of the water now, standing with the people down in front of the church. We were all together, breathing softly as we sang out and swayed close. When I listen to the Staple Singers, telling us to "see that host all dressed in red," I know we're all part of the crowd "that Moses led." Come on and follow me "down to the Jordan Stream."

Fifteen years earlier, a knife pushed forward and back into my mother's stomach; piercing the gut right through, it just missed the spine. That's all I know. Even when she told me the story of her doomed love, many years later, no details came through clearly, nothing but the flash of steel, the softness near the belly, and the relief she felt as she stabbed and the knife went deeply into her core. My mother never talked about what she suffered when she gave up the real love of her life. The young brother of her best friend, he had just returned from his junior year at the University of Georgia.

Through the haze of my father's mixture of care and complicity, which I somehow sensed, along with Lucille's expansive lies, I felt nothing. Lucille helped create a story that hid the attempted suicide. She told me that my mother had had an accident. I don't recall ever being taken to the hospital to see her. And when she came home, Lucille said that I looked as if "an evil spirit done took root in my body." By that time, Lucille and my father told stories about an ulcer. Belle, one of my mother's closest friends, invented another story that made the rounds: cutting open a box with the knife facing her, my mother lost control of it and stabbed herself accidentally in the stomach.

"Don't you worry about a thing," Lucille told me. "The doctors got her under good care. They took out that boil in her stomach." "Nothing but an ulcer," my father explained more than once. But I knew from rumors that my mother had done something bad, that she felt too guilty to live and hoped to die with a knife by her own hand. Years later, my mother did a kind of show-and-tell with me in my college dorm room. Looking at me with a smile, she told her story. Vexed by a break-up with that young lover, my mother drove a knife into her intestines and on through her back. "I just didn't want to live anymore. I loved him, but couldn't hurt your father." When she pulled it out, she fell flat out to the floor.

Lucille translated all the gossip and tribulation into something unexpected. She wanted me to know that blood was always a good sign. "The blood is the life. The soul of the flesh is in the blood." That's what Lucille said about the episode that seemed to cap my mother's ruined life. Breathing softly into my ear as our family fell slowly to pieces, she added: "God's gonna trouble the water." But no praise songs for the Lord or love songs between mere humans fully suited Lucille's sense of life. We needed to be reminded that we were animals. Until her death, she remained impatient with all the hooting and hollering about humans being close to heaven while other mammals on this earth could never lift up out of the dirt. "Step down. There ain't nothing wrong with dirt," she told me. "It's all we got, and we all gonna end up with the worms until we make it over to Jordan." From birth to death we're lowdown in it, she explained, and that's why we had to dip into water from time to time. "It sure gets dirty down here and we got to wipe off that stink." In my thirties, I tried.

Against the backdrop of my mother's despair and my own isolation appeared other near mystic but highly visible forces. Afraid of the white men with white hoods, I still wonder when I'll feel the shock of their presence in Nashville. I knew the killing stare that followed the mocking desire to frighten. Lucille warned me about the perpetual possibility of misfortune. Real terror plucks by the sleeve and comes along naturally, forever just occurring, always perceptible just at the edge of our vision. What terrorizes is the sheer malevolence of such long-time hate. Terror relayed not just by dogs, hoses, and bombs in the New South of the '60s, but by the near nonchalance of murder anywhere by any white person at anytime, in the dark of the night or at the break of dawn.

No matter where I go, and especially now, that fierce South stays with me, the dead look in the eyes of white sheriffs and the smiles on women's faces as they see dogs sicked on young black folks. There was no recourse and no one to turn to, except, for some, the Lord. But not for Lucille. The eyes turned toward heaven, the Amen of forgiveness, were not for her — instead the resigned knowledge that she held tight in her grin, a grin you might mistake for amusement, but was in fact restraint, a fury held back in the twist of the mouth. The twist was, now that I think about it, not quite a sneer and not quite a smirk. In that tightening of her lips lay a depth of understanding that came from years of holding back, standing tall, working hard for the very people who killed her own.

Out of the South

THE HOUSE HOLDS ME. On a gray winter morning, just as I was making plans to leave, a page appeared out of nowhere on the breakfast room table, the kind of paper I used years ago: Southworth Bond, 25 percent cotton and heavy weight. On the top, with a fountain pen, I had written, "Monday. Order *Harvard Literary Guide to the Bible*. Ed. Robert Alter and Frank Kermode." Then, three quarters way down the page in the same script and ink: "8/22/90. Thomas to Lucille: 'Do like a tack' (get lost)." But none of this matters, because in the center of the page in between these two notes, written in pencil in more or less the same script, but not quite, is a message to me. Off to the left on the page I found, and I can't figure out why, in small cramped pencil print: "Mom, reading from <u>Vogue</u>." Then to the right of it and running all the way down the page:

> Aug. 14 — delivered to me from
> "The stars are pushing you
> <u>to address important issues </u>

> this month. From Aug 24-Dec 20
> your ruling planet Jupiter goes out of
> phase which can cloud your judgment
> & slow your progress. It would be wise for
> you to take special care of your health &
> well-being through Dec. 20 because Jupiter
> is influencing those areas. Travelling or dealing w/
> foreigners may be unusually
> dramatic now. There will
> seldom be a dull moment for
> your sign this month.

Where did this come from? When did I write it? What did I mean when I wrote, "Mom, reading from Vogue"? These words from somewhere in the past I took to be a message from her, warning me as she always liked to. I'm superstitious. But more than that, I know there are spirits everywhere, the ghosts of the dead and the gods.

What did these words mean? Nothing has been the same. I am scared. The next day I awakened with pain in my back. I could not get up. I know my mother wants me right here, in the South, with her. When I finally got out of the bed, I felt as if something had scooped my bones into my gut. The dog seemed to be ill, too, lying around torpidly. I celebrated her birthday yesterday, two days after mine, in a state of suspension. Everything packed, and the suitcases and bags of books in the car. The large suitcases remain there still, but I've taken the food, my work, and a small suitcase out.

I sit in my study, emptied of everything except photos of my dogs and my god, along with his crosses, a necklace, and the three small stones given to me nearly 50 years ago by André Pierre. I will take the altar and everything on it along with me when I leave. I felt now more strongly than ever that I needed other spirits around me, good energy, not what I now felt was surely my mother's anger at the thought of my departure. Maybe I tried to placate her, with all the relics I cherished from Haiti.

I recalled meeting Pierre, an *oungan* and painter in Croix-des-Missions when I first went to Haiti nearly 50 years ago. Every time I returned to Haiti, I visited him. After the earthquake of 2010, I looked for him, hoping to find his *ounfo*. I headed out of Port-au-Prince on the short drive over a steel bridge to Croix-des-Missions, struck by seeing a lone goat in the dry riverbed. The Haiti I had returned to often and lived in since the summer of 1970, the last year of "Papa Doc" Duvalier's life, was unrecognizable: the number of *blancs* (whites or foreigners), the absence of vodou — no signs of the gods at the crossroads, no paint put down on the doors or sides of walls to call on the spirits of Guinea, and no drums heard in the night. So I decided to give respect to the dead, to the painter who first greeted me in 1970 and whom I last talked to in 1987, soon after the departure of the son, "Baby Doc" Duvalier. My driver and I had no trouble finding the turn, since even a very young man knew where to find Pierre's compound or *lakou*. The pigeons, chickens, and guinea hens no longer roamed the grounds, but the sacred trees (the *reposoirs* of the gods) still cast their dark, green shade over things. Pierre had died in 2005, at 91.

He could not paint, he told me, were it not for the *lwa* or spirits of vodou. "I paint with the hand of god," he said the last time I visited him. He never talked politics, even though we both smiled at the promise of "uprooting" or *dechoukaj*, now that the Duvalier family was gone. Instead, we talked about the gods. He told me about Ezili, known commonly as the "Black Venus" or "goddess of love." She is the spirit he served. Neatly displayed on the elaborately decorated dressing table that is her altar are three unopened bottles of wine (one labeled "Chateau de St Amour"), perfumes, basil leaves, a small lamp of oil, candlesticks, holy water, and a vase filled with white flowers. A Catholic chromolithograph, slightly tattered, leans against the wall: it depicts a young girl with a necklace of pearls and gold. Her heart is pierced with a yellow sword. When he was born, he was born for her, to be her *serviteur*. Not mere love or romance, but a promise of the most intense rendezvous, two nights alone with her every week. I get the impression when we talk that the room set aside for their time together is off limits. I might have been wrong, but I never asked him to open the door.

On this last visit, I did not find his family. An unidentified woman — I didn't ask who she was — led us to the *ounfo*. The light shone through the windows. It was his room, as well as the peristyle where the gods used to come. The blue walls were blue still, but that was all that remained except for the *poteau mitan*, the center post connecting the heavens to the earth and to the home of the gods under the water. Not one gourd, no liqueurs or perfumes, no *bagi* or altar, nothing else of color, no paint, only rubble. Nothing in the debris held the past, nothing was left of the jumble of objects, the objects usually kept apart turned into relics through practice, through handling and holding, giving power to the most common, the discarded, to become beautiful, to stun with their splendor.

But none of them are left. I stand in the debris with the light still coming through the windows, and the woman to whom I do not speak looks at me and opens the door to the room. I didn't want to be there, but I saw the bed. It is the bed where he slept with Ezili. It was still neatly made, the pillow at the top white, the room swept clean. I thanked her. The peristyle was shattered and neglected, but the room set aside for the god and her man was somehow preserved.

André Pierre, Ezili, the fiercely jealous Danbala, a wooden snake and one carved from stone, a glass of Haitian Rum Barbancourt, dark chocolate, a candle, an effigy made for me years ago: I gather from the desk where I write. My framed photo of the *veve* painted by Pierre I bumped with my elbow, and it came crashing to the floor, breaking the glass into splinters. Only half of the glass remained in the frame.

The weather had turned bitterly cold, and all along Interstates 81 and 95, the roads to the Northeast, accidents were occurring. At first, I joked that Trump's election "sent me into a state of anomie." Now I suspected the delay had more to do with things not of this world.

It was the house. My mother, just like the gods, did not want me to leave the South. Since she had no intention of coming with me, she knew how to hex my trip. I could see her laughing as she spoke the word *wanga*, which means something like sorcery, though that definition is too general. She always told me that somewhere somehow someone would curse me, in her words, "put the bad eye on you." I knew why I felt as if my head was stuffed with cotton wool and too heavy for my neck. I also knew that once "it's on you," there's nothing you can do, not if you believe.

The dead remain hidden in us. But from time to time they make themselves known. My mother was not subtle. White roses my husband bought for me turned brown. I slept too late in the morning, awakening around 8:30 or later. I almost fell down the stairs. I tripped over a root outside and caught myself just in time. I was afraid. Lucille watched over me as she always did, but I reckoned she also wanted me to stay put. Not in a mean, possessive way, not like my mother, but to keep me close to everything we love, so that she might remain part of that special life of bugs and dirt.

Stuck in the house, I heard something downstairs. A knock on the front door. A tall white man dressed in a suit stood outside. I asked what he wanted. I noticed that he had no brochures to sign or Bible to give away. I shouted through the door. I wouldn't open it. He said he just wanted to talk to me, and I said slowly, as if I wasn't sure of what would happen to my words: "I don't open the door to strangers." I went upstairs and tried to look out the windows of my study to see if he was still down below. "I'll stay up here," I thought to myself, sat down and put my head in my hands with exhaustion and dizziness. The dog was curled up but looking at me as if to reassure me that all would be okay. She still loves me, I know.

I was wearing an old blazer, a gray pinstriped flannel that I used to adore. It had been years since I wore it to out on the town, to a dinner or lecture. I had the odd sense that I'd been preparing for this trip North for such a long time that anything I used to do was more like a dream than a memory.

Maybe one can look forward to something for too long. Once too much time has passed, whatever had been desired turns into nothing more than a remnant from another life. It has nothing to do with anything real or knowable. Yes, that was it. "Jupiter goes out of phase," I muttered. The horoscope had become an omen, a gift from my mother: my judgment was clouded; any progress slowed. I found it, saw it on the table, as if it had always been right there, though I'd never seen it until then. What does it mean if a planet is out of phase?

Throughout my mother's life the press of objects meant everything to her. They piled up in her drawers. Lingerie became hiding places for jewels. Coat pockets held gold and diamonds, as well as pieces of licorice or pistachio nuts. She never threw anything away. Eyeliner, mascara, and all kinds of rouge and powder accumulated over the years, spreading into drawers that had been reserved for photos, charge cards, and address books. I had no idea how vital dead matter could be until the residue of my own life in Nashville surrounded me, occupying the kitchen, dining room, living room, bedroom and study. I list the places because these things are everywhere, and they know what they want.

They want to stay here with my mother. Maybe she's already claimed them as her own, just as she always tried to take everything I wanted most. I had a Steuben glass frog, I remember, given to me by my college roommate. My mother noticed it and liked it so much that one day, before she left my apartment, I gave it to her. When I visited her in Atlanta a few years later, I took it back. When she saw it on one of her visits, she took it without telling me. After she died years later, I saw it on her dresser, surrounded by perfume and cologne. A cycle of thievery.

On a leather chair in the den, my gray quilted down coat lazed on its back, spread out over the cushion holding two pairs of jeans, some underwear and a heavy white sweater. On the floor beside them, as if ready to jump up into their lap, was a pair of brown ankle boots. They were all waiting. These were not things my mother would want. She couldn't wear jeans, she said, since as she put it, rather sorrowfully: "They ride up funny into my crotch." But like everything else in this house turned upside down, they were all eager to head out.

It'd become a mausoleum. That's why I wanted to be gone, far away from dead things. Thomas the yardman had told me that ghosts walk around looking for what they have lost or left undone. My mother was here so that she could remain close to all the things that belonged to her: the bronze bust of a woman called (if you look at the inscription dug into the metal) "The

Woman of Flanders," dated "1914"; the Ming vase; silver candlesticks, paintings on the walls, crystal. Like the shell of a snail, all these things were as much a part of my mother's being as anything inside her. Or more, since they long ago became more real, more substantial than she. There are many forms of death.

The more I dismantled the house, moving things out to the car or packing them up or leaving some in wait for the moment when they too could leave, the less ready I was to go. Or to be clear, the more difficult it was for me to move. I was losing both energy and will. Pulled into the orbit of these inanimate objects, I too become heavy and still. Odd, but I bore no resemblance to the woman who had just a few days before leaned breathlessly into her reverie of ocean and her exaltation in everything that was not Nashville.

Black Pigs

IT WAS MY MOTHER'S Haiti that I carried with me, whether at home in the South or anywhere at all: the sacrificial food, liqueur, drum beats, blood, basil, and the braying of donkeys were there inside me, along with her ritual laughter. I recalled my mother hanging over the railing of a Hilton somewhere in the Caribbean, when I was very young, trying to pick mangoes. Though separated from Haiti and tempted into forgetting her life there, she shared with me, perhaps unwittingly, her attachment. I had to keep whatever she told me in mind, since everything she knew no longer existed. Destroyed by the earthquake of 2010, the neighborhoods where she was born and raised are in ruins. Nothing remains of her school Sacré Coeur, except a figure of Jesus on the cross in front of the collapsed church.

During every one of my visits to Haiti, and throughout the year I lived there, I never tried to find my mother's homes. Once she was dead, I wanted to see them, but it was too late. She lived in Bois Verna and Turgeau in the hills of Port-au-Prince. I had only a vague sense of what her homes looked like. When I asked her, she'd shake her head and run her fingers through her hair, saying, with a far-away look in her eyes, "beautiful, beautiful," as if just to remember them for a moment was the most extraordinary thing that she'd felt in a long time. At length, she'd describe a yellow gingerbread house with a red-peaked roof. She remembered the flamboyant railings of the second-floor gallery, where she and her brothers would take turns challenging each other to stand on the banister, sometimes balancing there as if in flight.

When I visited Haiti about six months after the earthquake, I felt as if I was walking slowly into my past, which always meant turning into my mother. In the bathroom near the boarding gate in Miami, I looked in the mirror and saw her in her best, most exquisite days, though I am heavier — I do not refuse to eat as often she did. "You can never be too skinny or too rich," she was unembarrassed to say. But the stiff elegance and tense look are hers, if not the stray hair, the unfinished face, and a walk that tells a story, always, no matter how many years have passed, of insecurity and fear.

Mixed in with her memory of rocks, lizards, and drums beating, pigs rooting, mangoes dripping, there was always the Virgin Mary, so pure that my mother winced when she thought about her and prayed, as she did so often at the end of her life, "Je vous salue Marie, pleine de grâce..." One night not long before she died, she told me again about the *djablesse*, but this time she described her weeping as she walked all alone in the night. Then she seemed anxious that I might not understand her, so she stopped, propped herself up on her pillows, and told me, "If you hear the howling wind, then you will see her. Her scream is not really a wail," she explained, "and it's quite different from any sound you ever heard. It comes and goes on the air." Unable not to repeat this story, she had turned it into a nightmare. My mother courted disaster hidden in the unexpected, in the most trivial things, just like her diamonds stashed deep into a jar of cold cream. Her premonitions of lust and secrets, I learned, could only maintain themselves in a glut of details, as if scum made to float on the surface of everything, so much so that I find myself still struggling for breath: the wicker baskets with mangoes rotting, crosses hidden in jiffy bags, lizards bleeding in the dirt, and the heads of cocks wrapped in mosquito netting.

Late, too late in my life, my mother shared with me this past that she had hidden; and once I became the vessel for her confidences, I felt even more a pretender. I had kept Haiti deep in my heart, my own secret place where I could go whenever I was most alone or cast aside by the outside world. But once I knew that she, the mother of such errant beauty, had been wrenched from Haiti, the only home she loved, I could never really catch up to life. Haiti was my own clandestine, treasured retreat, only to become a trap that would make me unable to ever be free of my mother. Continually I heard sniggering behind me. Was it my mother or the people around me, sensing my fakery? My spirit had been stolen; and the only way to regain what I had lost was to come out in some preposterous fashion as the little white girl who was really black, or, impossibly, the little black girl who had turned white.

When I was a child, my parents went on gambling junkets to Curaçao and Aruba, and always stopped in Port-au-Prince, bringing back paintings and sculptures. I became obsessed with a painting that portrayed a cow's head dripping blood, a dark brown finger stuck in a gourd, a little snake drinking blood from a dish, fruit on a table, a pelican head protruding from a knotted hole in a tree that wrapped around another tree, another bird's head severed, lying by the open bleeding meat of the cow's neck, a beetle, a red scarf gracefully flowing, pulled through a hole in a pitcher — all set before an opening onto a patch of terrain that appeared like a dream landscape of Haiti, blue skies, verdant hills, and a hut on exceptionally green turf.

They called it "Sacrifice." My father bragged that the artist Jacques-Enguerrand Gourgue was exhibited in the Museum of Modern Art in New York. That's what mattered to him, but I was drawn to it for different reasons. For hours I sat in front of this painting and begged my parents to give it to me. When I turned 16, it was mine. I took the painting to college and after that, put it on a wall of most everywhere else I lived. It is here with me now. Beneath it is the the altar for Danbala. Every morning I serve him espresso with brown sugar. After a run of unusually bad luck — another rib broken, one more tick bite, my dog slipping down the stairs, a tree that fell next to my house — I moved the altar downstairs into the living room.

I have made a home for my mother here in my way, not hers. This means not just living with snakes and spirits and jewels, but also what we left behind in Atlanta: the grit and meat of animal life, looking in the eyes of dogs, at the legs of spiders, entwined by the webs spun on the porch, in my study and bedroom, and expressing at last in our blood and sinews the flesh that we were meant to subdue.

My father hated animals. He kicked my puppy down the basement stairs, drowned the guinea pigs Ruben and Roddy, and shouted at my mother's canary whenever it sang for her. He didn't have to kill it, since it drowned in a glass of orange juice during breakfast. Early one morning, my mother had had enough of her husband's scorn for anything vibrant, what she called "physical life," and right before he died, she screamed out: "You're nothing but a *cochon blanc*." Then she beamed, as she muttered, "a white pig." He detested French too, and since he forbade her to use it whenever she tried, I never forgot this outburst. Later, she told me a story about pigs, the black pigs with the knowing eyes she grew up with. They were everywhere. She said she was "dazzled" by them. In the slanting light of late afternoon, the pigs, known also as "creole pigs," would come up to the garden in the rear of the house. They were smarter she said than anyone she had ever known, anywhere, and these pigs knew everything people tried to conceal.

My mother lived to see the slaughter of the Haitian black creole pigs in the early 1980s, when the US Health Department, warning about the dangers of a swine flu epidemic, helped annihilate them.. Thousands of peasants lost their hearty black pigs, their primary means of living. As one Haitian said, "When we lost our pig, we lost our bank account." The wholesale massacre turned out to be unnecessary. But that didn't matter. In 1984 new pigs arrived in Haiti by plane from the United States. What had happened, I asked. How would the Haitians be repaid? The

United States sent Haiti pink pigs from Iowa, called "white pigs" or "four-legged princes" by Haitians mourning for the loss of their pigs. Unused to the heat and the hard soil, these white pigs demanded special care.

Not used to foraging, they needed expensive feed and elaborate cages that were out of the sun, since, as one Haitian told me, "they have soft stomachs, delicate feet, and thin skin." These pigs either died or ended up in the various Protestant missions that sprang up in the late 1980s. When I returned in 1986, there were only a few black pigs left. It was a violent time, just after the departure of Baby Doc and the rest of his family on board a United States Air Force C-141 jet. During the days of "uprooting," I heard about unreported attacks on vodou — the destruction of local culture played out as a ritual of revolution. Temples were desecrated, priests killed, hacked to death, or forced to swallow gasoline and then set on fire. But the black pigs brought everything into focus: their murder seemed ghoulish, leaving me aware of how blood coursed over the land, along with the lament of the people who cared for and loved them.

When I visited "Christianville," a mission founded by the First Christian Church, the pastor took me to a pig farm established for the new imported white pigs, turned into booty for those Haitians who turned their backs on vodou and took Christ into their hearts. One farmer complained to me that white pigs were "prize pigs." The only way you'd get one of these "four-legged kings" was "to walk away from your land and crawl into a white world." According to the *Evangel*, "a Christian Quarterly from the Caribbean," each farmer, once converted from what the pastor called "witchcraft," got one white baby sow. "Pigs, pigs, pigs. The pig house is full of them. And pretty soon our big fat mothers will give us lots more pigs. Out in the mountains are many children waiting for their daddies to have pigs, too." But the pigs could not live on the peasants' land. So Haitians had to come to the mission to see their pigs. They never again had pigs on their land. In a couple of years, most of them had lost their land, anyway.

When I told my mother this story, she looked at me but said nothing. Hours went by. At last, I heard her call me from her bedroom. She sat bolt upright and still, shut her eyes, and said in a whisper, "I used to pull the tail of one little black pig, and she loved it." I asked her what happened to it, and she talked about men, "the men who hate the things we love, even the shade of trees, the sound of hooves." To this day I cannot really explain how I did not stay right there by her side and listen, asking for more words, more of her remembered past. Instead, since she had already turned away, I left her in the darkened room without saying a word. After my father died, she moved only one painting out of the living room and into her room of white silk and lace sheets with antique white furniture and gold gilt. It was Wilson Bigaud's painting of a peasant and his black pig with the curling tail. Painted about 20 years before the eradication program began, this portrait captured the Haiti my mother knew.

The flesh with or without blood, I thought, when my mother, pale from loneliness and heart problems, asked me to give her the shot of Coumadin that would prevent strokes and blood clots in her veins and arteries. I remembered how she sliced into her stomach with a knife, and decided that I would find the path of the scar, placing the needle for each injection along it. The life is the blood, I kept telling myself. But she talked about *baka*, the red-eyed evil spirits that sucked blood deep into the night, and recalled how she heard their barks, whinnies, and bellowing first as a child in Haiti and again now every time she closed her eyes. "Too many dead things," she told me, "rooting around out back. I hear them rummaging in the mud and calling out to me." I thought then about our yard not as a plot of earth but as the water road, the *chemin d'leau*, where the spirits go. "The dead do not die, they go under the waters." What kind of prayers, I wondered, could we offer to the unquiet dead, majestic animals coming up unexpectedly out of the waters? I tried to pray aloud, asking my mother to join me. Instead, she laughed and chanted in a singsong, somewhat mocking voice: "Find the dog with a stick in its mouth and lead it to water. Light up the night, take the stick, and drown the dog."

Her words never left me. I thought about the bloated dog. I looked at my mother and remembered with a jolt how she once told me that her family lived in Port-au-Prince next door to Nicole and Jacques Roumain. Jacques was a brilliant ethnographer and defender of vodou and author of *Les Gouverneurs de la rosée* (translated by Langston Hughes as *Masters of the Dew*), a searing story of the peasant struggle in Haiti. Roumain always took time to talk to her, she said, and when kids shouted at her "*gadé kochon pwal*" (Look at her hairy pig legs), he would put a stop to their taunts. But it was to be another few days into our private ceremonial, with her lying down as she waited for me to come and visit her, before I heard — as if she had finally decided to finish her story from years before — about that old, and now recollected taunt: "I didn't shave yet, so my black hairs reminded them of black creole pigs, I guess." Then she looked at me and added, "We're in a hole. I cannot exactly catch onto the rope to get out without hurting you. So we'll never find each other, but maybe there are other ways to make our lives mean something when words are dead." In no time at all, she was asleep. All I saw for days were legs, with her or without her, the prickly flesh, the black hairs that seemed so desolately soft and dying, in her dimly lit room.

In the Belly of Her Ghost

MY MOTHER IS IN my house in Nashville, hovering around her things. How else can I understand why things disappear or fall off shelves, or why Stella, eyes opened wide, starts peeing at the top of the stairs, on the oriental rug, or at my bedroom door? Maybe my mother wants me to know that because I have her things, she has earned the right to possess me. She wants to be closeted inside my body just like the things she once hoarded in her bedroom drawers.

Surrounded by these relics of her existence, still in boxes in my basement and garage, I am losing things. Or have I forgotten where I put them? Every morning when I awaken, I notice that something has disappeared. Like the shell of a snail, all these objects, the paintings that were once on her walls, the crystal and silver on her tables, were as much a part of my mother's being as anything inside her. I should have known. I longed for her things as if they might magically transform my childhood irrelevance. My mother and I had made an exchange, a devil's bargain. Our lives required a circuit of possession. She demanded things from my father and then I prodded her to pass them on to me.

Things, like ghosts, know what they want. I gave away my mother's evening gown and jacket, covered in blue and white sequins. I was relieved when it was gone. She had kept it for forty years. I remembered how it held her body in its weight and beauty. The dress was more alive than my mother's smile. It not only held her tight but also seemed to live for her, giving up its shine so that her frozen smile could come alive and sparkle. Hanging in the wardrobe box next to other boxes in my garage, the dress felt warm when I removed it. I hesitated, thinking I should keep it as a memento. But I alternated between fear of giving her something to inhabit and concern that in giving it away I was discarding her. After the Goodwill truck left — boxes filled with linens, wine goblets, furs, suits, coats, and gowns including this, the most beautiful one — I walked back to the garage. There on the floor lay a small sequined belt. I picked it up and held my mother's tight little waist in my hand.

It is not easy to tell a ghost story that is not meant to frighten. How can I summon this woman who now dead has decided to give herself to me? Perhaps this is not a ghost story, just the urging of an unquiet spirit who wants me to remember her skin, who wants me to know each day how strongly her hand held mine, pulling me into her secrets, teaching me to know that my home would soon be hers.

She tried hard to make things live. She accumulated them, handled them, sought them and kept them, thinking that if she treasured them enough she might create vitality where there was none. Was there something in her manner of cherishing that made her sense that she was still alive, even when everything was dying within her?

I killed my mother by taking away her things. I began the dispossession while she was still in Atlanta. The house had to be sold, but it was filled with junk. My dolls still lay in the basement side by side in a long white box. As a child I had preferred frogs and spiders to dolls, which I mutilated as Lucille watched. She hated prettiness and warned me about "the fandangles" that kill — she loved that word for embellishment and used it for all kinds of things: she called women who wear make-up "nothing but fandangles," and when I wasted time or messed around, she accused me of "fandangling." Though the dolls' lace dresses remained intact, their hair had been cut or shaved off; and their eyes, which I had not hurt, had rotted, as if they had been eaten away by acid. No eyeballs remained. I told Thomas the yardman to throw them out. My mother came downstairs and asked with wonder, "But, don't you want to keep your dolls?"

It was all about keeping and losing. I hired an expert to do an estate sale while my mother was still in Atlanta. I could not be there, since I was in the midst of a move myself. But before I left, I threw away bills dating from the '60s and collected books to take to Goodwill. My mother went from room to room, making sure that I touched nothing of my father's. Though he had been dead nearly 10 years, she told me that he never left her alone for too long and reminded me "how awful he'd feel when he visited and saw that there was nothing left for him to wear."

She hid her silver. She carried to the pantry the small painting of Moses and his tablets and the strange portrait of two little Italian boys holding fruit. I had already returned to my home in Philadelphia, where I had just begun teaching, when she complained on the phone: "I am all alone. Those women you found treated me like dirt. You left me with total strangers. They didn't answer me, didn't let me know the prices of my things. They sold everything for nothing." She was never herself after the things left the house. Even though they were part of what I supposed trivial — discolored leather valises, unused linens, random trifles, odds and ends of costume jewelry, worn-out crockery and motley souvenirs — something had been knocked out of her.

She couldn't find the silver and paintings she had hidden. Her voice changed to a whisper. Perhaps I caused her unraveling by making her part with the things that held her together, images that told her who she was, giving her the lineaments of worth. I took the old paintings that were for me the core of my father's art collection: the portrait of St. Catherine and the head of St. John carried by Salome. I wanted a very large Ming vase, but she would not let me have it. Did the blue and white figures nearly floating in the trees that reached to the clouds recall to her something of the feeling she had lost after leaving Haiti?

The very thought of parting with things seemed to provoke her demise. She asked me if I wanted her to die, telling me: "I'm not dead. But when I am, you will have it all." Perhaps I wanted her things more than I knew. I must have believed that if she gave me things I would be sated, graced with fulfillment, forgetting that she felt as empty as I. Things had given her only a sham respite from what she called "our curse."

"May it therefore be Thy Will, O Lord, our God and God of our fathers, to forgive us all our sins." On September 27, 2001 on the Jewish Day of Atonement, when God's book of judgment is closed and sealed, my mother disappeared somewhere between the doctor's office and her home in Buckhead. She was invited to break the fast at her friend Nora's house, and when she didn't appear, Nora called me in Philadelphia. Worried, I called the police. I learned that there was no car at the house and no sign of my mother. A day later, sitting in the one habitable room of the row house I had just bought on Naudain Street in Center City, while electricians, painters, carpenters, and plumbers fought it out downstairs, I finally heard from my mother's doctor. "Your mother was found passed out in a corner of the parking lot at Kroger's. She's in the hospital and can't leave until you get to Atlanta. She can't be alone," he said. "You must come."

I got in the car and drove for two days straight, along with my dog, a gentle Rottweiler, "Dogie," named for the orphan calves (also known as "dough-guts") in my father's favorite song, "Git along little dogies." At the hospital, my mother lay in bed, and fixing me with her eyes, she followed my words with her lips. I wondered where her friends had gone. The old friends she had so loved never appeared at the hospital or at her house. Her memory was going. She knew me, but she no longer knew which keys opened the door of her home. For the first time I noticed something new in my mother's behavior. She kept looking at her watch. The Cartier no longer worked, but she kept setting it. What would become just one of her rituals had begun. "What time is it?" "Oh, it stopped." With each repetition, sometimes twice in an hour, she would rewind the watch. For two weeks after she left the hospital, we stayed in Atlanta in the house that still had not sold.

Morning and night, I gave my mother pills with sonorous names: estratest, lanoxin, synthroid, maxzide, betapace, zestril. Every day I gave her a shot of lovenox in the fat of her belly. "It's 30 mg. of something subcutaneous morning and evening, plugged quickly into her to prevent clotting," the nurse explained. We visited the doctor one last time before leaving together for Philadelphia. He told me about my mother's heart, the bad rhythm, the torn chordae, the leaking valve, the irregular beat, the blood collecting in a pool, the lack of blood to the brain, the short-term memory loss, the possible beginning of Alzheimer's. Then, knowing that my mother would probably not see her home again, I lied and reassured her that she would visit me briefly until she got better and returned to Atlanta.

In Philadelphia, my mother dropped used Kleenex all over the house. She smiled, and kept repeating: "I don't want to be a burden on you." After a week, she insisted on going to the grocery store on South Street, a couple of blocks away. I drew a map for her, and made sure she understood the way back home. The first time she did not return, I found her turning a corner on Lombard Street. She must have been making that turn for a long time, since she'd already been gone over an hour. She kept going back to the grocery. Every afternoon, more cans of tuna, sesame crackers, and mangoes appeared on the kitchen counter. The pile grew. The kitchen had been gutted before I moved in. Only the wooden counter remained. She brought to it what she had always loved. Mangoes accumulated.

She stopped eating. I watched her ceremonies of accumulation and denial and began buying different kinds of food that I knew she liked. She ate one bite of salad. That was it. I took her to dinner. She had a peculiar relation to the things on the table, as if she no longer remembered what to do with them. I stared at the whites of her eyes. They had turned a strange ivory color. She lost her lipstick. I found half of it in the wash. A second week passed. We made two trips to the emergency room late at night when she had difficulty breathing. During these times, sitting in the bright cubicle for hours, she told me that her flesh had become "food for maggots."

I watched her closely, trying to know where she had gone, into which details she had put her faith. Her old habits remained, but seemed deliberately exaggerated. The toss of her head, the slow smile, the coy innuendo the same, but something had happened to her hair, the lipstick was too red, and her jokes no longer made sense. Then her mood changed. "I'll just kill myself. I see it in your eyes. You hate having me here." When I asked my mother "Where do you want to go?" she answered, "To heaven."

I did not want to love her as much as I did. When I was a child she made it clear that she needed to shake off my attachment, hold her ears against it as if trying to avoid finger nails scraping across the blackboard. Much later, when I was in college, away from home, she apologized for hurting me. She'd take me into her bedroom, open her lingerie drawers, and take out the piles of cards and letters I had written her. For years they had been kept, tied together with ribbons and buried in the folds of her silk and satin. Surprised, I held the proofs of my longing for her, the Valentine, Christmas, and birthday cards I had made. Painted hearts with ribbons, poems composed about eternal love and apologies for being "bad," whatever that word then meant to me.

I had not kept track of the excesses of my adoration. As I grew older love turned readily into hate that I controlled and limned for dramatic effect. Docile longing turned into litanies of blame. Abandoned and unloved, I told stories that turned my mother into a mirror that reflected my uniqueness. But sometimes alone in the night I wondered about the possible effects of dishonoring her. Did words have power to harm? She had always told me that bad thoughts could kill.

She felt my father didn't love her enough. I punished her for not loving me enough. She was wrong about my father. Was I mistaken about her? "Treat me like a person," she pleaded to my father, who never allowed her to be independent, who had turned her into a thing of great value. "Stop talking about me without naming me. You're calling me 'she' again." The decay I watched during her last five years had already begun long before I took part in its growth. Though admired as beautiful, she belonged to my father — his icon of tenuous perfection. How tiring it must have been. A machine of femininity, a token of luxury, she began to run down. Finally, in her last year, she hunched over and stopped talking. After shuffling for a few months, she stopped walking. But she never forgot the lure of things, lamenting that she didn't have anything to give me: no money, no gifts.

Her sisters in Brooklyn decided that I could not care for her and made plans for her to return to the place where she had lived as a teenager, six blocks down from her old house on Ocean Parkway. I could not stop Jamie, the sweet-talking Trinidadian caretaker from tying my mother to the bed to prevent her from getting up during the night, and the sisters insisted that I was making trouble, as always.

Until my mother died, just two years later, she used to walk around the apartment, touch the silver and crystal, look at each painting, open and close the drawers in the three bedrooms of her apartment. Later, she hid silverware in lingerie. I only discovered the forks and spoons and knives and ladles after she died. They had been removed from the mahogany box and secreted away. I never found the box. Then I found my diamond ring hidden in her cold cream. She had taken it from the dresser in the guest room sometime during the night.

The less her body worked, the more I felt her take me into her. I would lie down beside her, put my head on her shoulder and run my fingers through her hair. When her sisters allowed their doctor to put a feeding peg in her stomach without my knowledge, my mother went into cardiac arrest. My mother had fought him, he said, as he tried to put the scope down her throat. I flew to New York for the third time in four weeks. She lay in the ICU unit. All DNR ("do not resuscitate") instructions I had given the hospital had been ignored, or, as the nurses put it, "rescinded," because of the emergency in the operating room. I saw her with a central line in her neck, a respirator, feeding tube, heart monitor, catheter, and intravenous lines. She looked at me and took my hand. Knowing how she felt about doctors and intrusive medical tactics, I recalled what she said when we visited Elaine's runaround husband Bernard, the man who used to fondle her those quiet afternoons on the sofa in Atlanta. "Well, she sure got back at him, shoving that tube in his nose and down his throat. Poor guy, what a way to go."

I flew back and forth between Brooklyn and Nashville, getting her out of the hospital and back to her apartment, where Jamie cared for and also humiliated her. I tried to save my mother. Was I saving myself? I wanted to move her out of harm's way, away from a family crazed in denial, who wanted her to remain in the hospital, pierced with needles, kept alive with tubes, always accessible, an object they could adore. "She's beautiful, like a doll." "Look, she's smiling." Dispossessed of her things, my mother had now been turned into a thing, locked in this gruesome masquerade.

We are having a conversation. We talk a lot now, as we never did when she was alive. I can't forget how I let her eyes go, never replaced her glasses. The old ones sat in her top drawer. I only realized recently why she had stopped reading the newspaper. We were all so ready to believe she was demented. She was not; she was waiting to see how she would be treated, if the horrors she had imagined would be true now that she was losing her looks, now that her hair had turned gray and always looked damp. She kept looking in the mirror. Her sisters kept putting makeup on her: first eyeliner, then mascara, eye shadow a dusky blue, and only then came the foundation and rouge. She looked as if she had been embalmed; and after they left, as I removed it all with cold cream, she smiled.

Why didn't I replace her glasses? It was as if I wanted to let her go, fold into nonexistence. But she was too strong for that, and instead began to sing. Even if she could no longer speak in sentences, she remembered the songs that she loved; and through them she returned to her first years in New York. She sang fragments, usually the first lines, a bit off key, as if part of a conversation she held on to. Whenever I got ready to leave after a visit, she repeated, now as a command, "Baby, it's cold outside."

Early one Monday morning, right after my last trip to Brooklyn, only five days after I had removed her from the hospital and returned to Nashville, a cousin I hardly knew came to my mother's apartment and called an orthodox Jewish ambulance service named "Hatsalah" (Hebrew for "rescue"). In traditional Jewish law, the inestimable value of human life — and its preservation — trumps suffering. Even if motivated by love or compassion, you cannot let a person die peacefully at home, as my mother's hospice aides had hoped. Such a death is tantamount to murder. After threatening to call the police, the volunteer driver denounced the registered nurse, the caretaker, and the hospice worker. Then, for the fourth time that summer, my mother was removed against my wishes, to New York Community Hospital on King's Highway in Brooklyn. Since we had all followed the instructions of her cardiologist at Mt. Sinai, my aunt persisted in calling us "killers." But no matter: in my absence, the emergency volunteers on the ambulance flooded her with liquids, though she could no longer swallow.

Two days later, at around 5:20 in the afternoon, she died. Her heart stopped as dusk fell. I was in an East Nashville parking lot, right outside a health food grocery when my cell phone rang. Tired from my first day of teaching, I let it ring but then realized that I'd better pick it up to hear a nurse tell me the news. I sat in the car. Then I went on to my yoga class, since I was afraid to go home where, alone, I'd be drawn too powerfully outside in the backyard as night fell. That's where she'd want me to be, alone with her laughter, hearing her footsteps on the soft brown soil.

When I returned home the phone rang and rang. I took my dogs for a walk. When I returned, I slowly picked up the phone. As if in a trance, I heard a disembodied voice tell me the story of what had happened to my mother. It was a Rabbi, one of the men my mother called "black hats" that she feared. Convinced that they were always masturbating, she said there was nothing more terrifying than that not-so-hidden vice. To hear her tell it, you had to be careful if you stopped at a red light in Brooklyn. When you looked over into the next car, that ultra-orthodox man of the cloth might just be grinning at you while he showed you his penis. So I listened to this Rabbi on the phone tell me that one of the sisters' sons had claimed to be my mother's only son. I must have screamed. I know that I said my mother had no son. But it was too late. With that pretense, the nephew persuaded another Rabbi to remove my mother from the hospital and get her as far away from me as possible.

I heard from no one in the family, just this Rabbi who told me he had the body and would prepare it for a funeral that the sisters had planned. All I could think of were two strangely incongruent things: my mother's conviction that every orthodox Rabbi "whacked their penis," and the writ of habeas corpus. I shuddered when I heard the meaning reverberate in my head: you have the body; you have the body. Dating all the way back to Magna Carta, the writ guarantees that no one can be imprisoned or restrained without due process of law. But my mother was not only locked up in that house in Brooklyn, what remained of her had also been taken.

"A stolen body, a secret funeral," these words kept going through my mind, "a jingle, a jangle," as I made numerous calls in order to get my mother home. I wanted her back in Atlanta so that she could be buried in her plot beside my father. When I agreed to pay for the first, illegitimate funeral costs, she was put on a plane to Atlanta. There, after another funeral, attended by only a few people, including her stockbroker and her doctor, I watched as her pinewood coffin was lowered into the dirt of the South.

But she didn't linger in decay next to her husband in that earth. Instead, she shone in her spirit and traveled here to Nashville. I hear Lucille telling me, "She done come back where she belongs. No way she'd stay away from you." Only in retrospect did I realize that it was inevitable. During the last 10 years of her life, she asked, "When are you coming home?" or insisted, "I'll always be with you. We'll always have each other. I would do anything for you." I asked her repeatedly, during those two years in Brooklyn, if she wanted to return to the South, the place she loved. She never answered me, even though she still talked and answered other questions. Maybe she knew that she would be here soon enough, in her way not mine.

I had no idea how vital dead matter could be until the residue of my mother's life arrived in Nashville: not only the oil-splattered recipe books, golf trophies, and bunches of keys, but, let me repeat, paintings, silver, crystal, furs, the clothes and boxes upon boxes of photos that my father had taken of her in every pose, dressed or undressed, night and day. I stood in my garage. I caressed my mother's dresses. Yes, the gowns handmade in China and India covered with sequins, pearls, and lace. I try to lift one of the gowns on its hanger. It is very heavy. I can hardly get it out of the box. I wonder how she could have worn it. "Like a harem girl," I heard a man say one night as she entered the living room of the old house in Atlanta, while I hid in the hall outside, listening and watching.

I called Roz Balser one morning after my mother died. She was my mother's best friend. My mother had counted on Roz when she and my father moved to the little house with the steep driveway on Briarcliff Road. About 94 when we spoke, she was 11 years older than my mother. I caught her in the Jacuzzi tub, soaking in oatmeal salts. "I got this damned dry skin," she said. Roz had promised me just after my mother's death that she would tell me about the early days in Atlanta. I hoped to connect the fragments of the life she offered to me a week after my mother was buried. "Your mother loved you." "It was a tragic life." "Life wasn't good for Frenchie." So I asked her why my mother was unhappy. In a drawl, she responded as if from a script too often repeated. "She gave too many gifts, she was too generous. That was the problem. People took advantage of her. Nobody understood her. But she never complained, no matter what." I wanted to know if she caused bad things to happen to her or were these occurrences beyond her control. But since Roz had to get out of the tub, she quickly ended our conversation, saying: "Maybe we're better off not knowing."

How could my mother have lived so long in one place and be so forgotten? Not so much forgotten, but made insubstantial, disposable. She was not missed by her friends in Atlanta, but I missed her. I always felt her absence, though even in her presence I felt as if she was not there. She spoke in parables, taunting me with talismans of what I one day might need to know, but not yet, not now. "I saw your father last night. He was up in the ceiling, near the light."

When I was a child, I kept having a dream that has not faded away. Someone drove me to a dump not far from our house in Atlanta. Covered with kudzu and filled with stones, the place was encircled by leafless trees. Whoever took me to the dump left me there in the dark of night. I stumbled over pieces of iron, broken glass, and electric wires. Since I was afraid to touch the garbage that might have stopped my fall, I kept landing on my face. I opened my eyes, saw a clutter of objects, and stumbled again. Boxes of clothes, paintings huddled together, toilet bowls, mink coats, and refrigerator doors. I looked up from the ground. I had become part of the rubbish. I had been thrown away.

The things and my mother conspire together against me. Whatever I thought precious, all the objects that I had been so glad to possess have gathered in my home as instruments in my destruction. I don't like to look at the paintings, and I can't wait to get rid of the silver and crystal. What had been beautiful in her home has turned into debris in mine. But my mother's spirit is stunning. We might yet make something out of all the wrong done.

Spider Mama

SHE ANSWERS ME. Still, in the morning, hanging by a thread at the edge of the window, she moves when I call her, "Hey, mother," with a lilt and depth that surprise me. No mere movement, but a fast twirl. That is her greeting, just as when she came down from the light in my study. In and out of focus she goes whenever I take her photo. When I return after a couple of hours and speak to her again, she turns round and round. I wonder whether it's my breath that moves her as if a rush of wind. So I move away and call to her from a distance. She seems to pulsate and then turns at a peculiar angle before stirring again, so that her front legs incline towards me, with an alacrity that unnerves me.

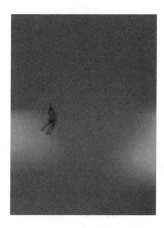

All day she remains suspended, moving only when I come near and speak. Now, as I get ready to go to bed, I look over, and she's still hanging by that line, dangling, not weaving a web. Without a web, she can't catch food, but she has no reason to eat. I wonder if she'll die, and then I realize that she's already dead.

"I've got the world on a string." I hear my mother's favorite song when I was young, and "Let's face the music and dance," which in her teens she had seen Ginger Rogers sing, all gossamer in white, with such elegance, lifted up by Astaire, heels and lace, flutter and fur, all awash in whiteness. In death, she continues to summon these songs, these images: the dead end of my mother's dream, a first and a final turning away from her self — the raw sensuality that was hers—and into the frozen and counterfeit dream of white flesh. "Why not," she sang, "take all of me?"

Acclaim for *In the Belly of Her Ghost*

In times such as ours, and the times from which they spawned, ages of violence against all forms of "other" — genders, bodies, skins, ideas — how can we lay to rest the ghosts that haunt us, and invite to the table those that help us live?

Writing from the headlands far into the interior, threading the personal with the public, an elegy with a covert manifesto of hope, Colin Dayan understands what it is to be haunted: by history, by race, by family, by what presses on the definitions of one's life.

In pages at once strikingly evocative, allusive, and embodied, rigorously sensory in their hard-won wisdoms, Dayan argues for the co-existence of species, variants of identity and belonging, a commonwealth of the living and the dead.

In the Belly of Her Ghost imbues profound remembering with a democracy of looking and listening, where all that matters — objects, animals, people and place — is properly attended. It is a volume appearing undeniably in its necessary moment, and it is precisely necessary because the truths it speaks are as old as our troubles, as required as our joys.

— Andrea Luka Zimmerman

This subtle, ambivalent, deeply thoughtful book makes nothing easy — difficult moments are imbued with grace and familiar parades of ghosts. We hear a series of conversations: with the past, with selves old and new, with memories of Haiti and the American South, with a black woman who effectively mothered the writer, with an actual mother both dead and alive. How many of us could so lucidly say of a disappointed and disappointing parent, "I did not want to love her as much as I did"? At the center of this haunting narrative is an unforgettable ghost story, which, ultimately, is not quite a ghost story at all.

— Michael Wood

I sat rapt, coiled tensely around myself, awaiting I didn't know what exactly, nothing I could put a name to, but something I felt a fierce identification with, an anxious anticipation, a premonition of dread, a shroud of sorrow, a life encompassed by secrets.

In The Belly of Her Ghost is a soul story that resonates in the body of anyone who has been or is cast out of anywhere she calls home. It's allusive, elusive; its strength is its narrative freedom from story as we know it. Its brilliance in earth shimmers (I will never again think of a summer night in nature in any other way). Its time is archetypal, images, ideas, affects evanesce and return. For this country is timeless.

— Wendy Lochner